The Successful Family Business

A Proactive Plan for Managing the Family and the Business

Edward D. Hess

 PRAEGER

Westport, Connecticut
London

Library of Congress Cataloging-in-Publication Data

Hess, Edward D.
  The successful family business : a proactive plan for managing the family
and the business / Edward D. Hess.
      p.   cm.
  Includes bibliographical references and index.
  ISBN 0–275–98887–2 (alk. paper)
  1. Family-owned business enterprises—Management. 2. Family-owned
business enterprises—Management—Case studies. I. Title.
  HD62.25.H47 2006
  658'.045—dc22   2005019269

British Library Cataloguing in Publication Data is available.

Library of Congress Catalog Card Number: 2005019269
ISBN: 0–275–98887–2

First published in 2006

Praeger Publishers, 88 Post Road West, Westport, CT 06881
An imprint of Greenwood Publishing Group, Inc.
www.praeger.com

Printed in the United States of America

The paper used in this book complies with the
Permanent Paper Standard issued by the National
Information Standards Organization (Z39.48-1984).

10 9 8 7 6 5 4 3 2 1

With thanks and love to the memories of
Jack Hess and
Coach Charles Grisham.
And to my wife, Katherine.

Contents

Introduction

Family businesses are a major part of the U.S. economy. Eighty percent or more of all businesses in the United States are family controlled. Over 60 percent of the U.S. workforce works for a family business.[1] Family businesses embody our country's entrepreneurial spirit and represent the hopes and dreams of many for independence, community, self-sufficiency, and wealth.

Likewise, in Europe and South and Central America, family businesses dominate the economic structure and control significant parts of the economies of many countries. Thus, family businesses are an important part of our global economy.

Family businesses are owned by families—groups of related individuals, each with their own unique mixture of values, history, and emotional relationships. Through the family business some families seek continuity, closeness, a sense of community, and belonging to something meaningful.

Unfortunately, the success rate of most such entrepreneurial businesses in general are poor. Estimates are that 70–80 percent of all private businesses fail during the first four to five years of existence and fewer than 10 percent last ten years. Family business statistics show that fewer than one third of them pass successfully to a second generation.

This book's focus is the family business—any business that has or will have two or more generations or two or more family branches either working in the business or owning the business. What makes family businesses different from non-family businesses is the added complexity of family dynamics that cause most family businesses to operate, to adopt strategies, and to make decisions differently. Families factor in family needs, hopes, and fears into their decisions regarding the business and only family businesses have sibling or cousin rivalries, jealousies, and competition for parental love, approval, and financial favor. Family dynamics, family ways of communicating and making decisions all can interfere with business decisions. This is the beauty of and challenge of managing a family business.

Being a family business leader carries the responsibility of not only managing the business but also of managing the family dynamics if you want the family business to be successful. And what is success for a family business? A successful family business is a successful business that does not destroy or lessen family harmony.

Successful family businesses do not let the family destroy the business or the business destroy the family.

Throughout this book, we will focus on five recurring themes:

1. Your chances of having a successful family business will be greater if you proactively and preemptively manage *both* the business and the family.

2. In order to manage a family business successfully, you need to accept the fact that there will be reoccurring family business issues; that is, family issues that will impact the business, or put financial pressures on the business, and business issues that will impact each family member differently. The issues will change as the family expands and as the family ages because family members' emotional and financial needs will change as their life circumstances change. These issues are predictable and occur in most family businesses.

3. In managing family business issues, you need an analytical framework or template that takes into account the differing, changing perspectives of the business, the family, and the non–family member employees and shareholders, if any.

4. To successfully manage a family business, you need a process by that you can manage the surfacing of and the debate of family business issues; and

5. That process should be based upon and reinforce the key values that are most important to you and your family. Family values will be an overriding factor in mitigating jealousies, rivalries, and personal financial self-interest.

A family and a business are two dynamic, evolving, changing organisms—each unique—each with their own history, challenges, strengths, weaknesses, opportunities, and threats. A family business is the interaction of these two dynamic organisms.

Family issues will interact and overlap with the business. The family will impact the business. Because of that impact, most family businesses operate differently than non-family businesses. The business will also impact

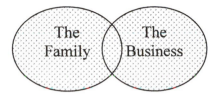

Figure I.1. The Overlap

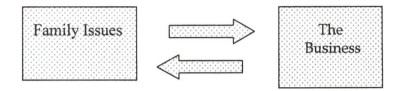

Figure I.2. Impacts

the family since family members' livelihoods, financial security, status, and community standing are derived from the business.

It is rare for a family and a business to be static. Something is always changing. Family members are aging—going to college, getting married, having children, buying homes, getting older, sick, and divorced. Likewise, the business is changing—new competitors, employees quitting, customers changing, and growing pains.

It is this constant change—evolution of the family and evolution of the business—that creates a continuous flow of family business issues that need to be managed in order to increase the probability of the business remaining successful and the family remaining harmonious.

Not only are the family and the business two different evolving dynamic organizations but each is made up of different constituents or members. Family members include the founders of the business, family shareholders, their children, their grandchildren, and spouses, some of whom may work in the business and some of whom may not; some of whom may own stock in the family business and some of whom may not. Likewise, the business will likely have non-family member employees and may have non-family member shareholders whose interests can impact the business and the family.

The complexity of the issues and the different perspectives of individuals involved will depend upon their various roles in the family and in the business. It is this dynamic and these different perspectives that present the challenges of managing a family business.

It is this challenge—the challenge of managing both the business and the family—that is the theme of this book and the reason it was written. This book is written for family business founders, family shareholders, family employees, family members not working in the business, family business directors, independent directors, and for non-family management, shareholders, and key employees.

This book will discuss all of the following commonly occurring family business issues:

- Which family members should work in the business? How should they be compensated? How should their performances be reviewed?
- Who should own stock in the family business? What happens to that stock when someone experiences a divorce? How is the business impacted by a death in the family? To whom can the stock be transferred?
- Should the family business pay dividends? Should the family business have a stock buy-back plan?
- Who should serve on the Board of Directors?
- How do you choose a successor CEO? When should the successor be a family member? When should the successor be an outsider (non-family member)?
- For family shareholders not working in the business, what are their equitable benefits? How do you keep them involved or connected to the business?
- What family members can attend shareholders meetings? Who gets told what? And when?

Most family business issues fall into one of the following four categories:

1. Inter-generational (between different generations) equity, financial, and control issues;
2. Intra-generational (within one generation) equity, financial, and power issues;
3. Family member favoritism or privileges versus arms-length market business dealings;
4. Jealousies and rivalries with family members competing for recognition, love, and money.

I have spent most of my career working with private family companies. First as a lawyer, secondly as an investment banker, and lastly, as a consultant. This book is the culmination of all those learning experiences over the past 30 years and to the many clients from whom I have learned, I say thank you. Examples in this book are true and based on real events—I have changed the names and states and generalized to maintain and ensure confidentiality. The principles discussed and issues faced are reoccurring, common issues likely to be faced by all family businesses.

You can learn from others' experiences. Most family businesses face similar issues and challenges. And the issues and challenges are predictable as families age and grow. We also will learn from highly publicized family disputes. One of my purposes is to share with you what I have seen work well and what has not worked well. But the advice herein will not guarantee success.

I hope you come away with four changes in how you approach family business issues:

1. Your MINDSET—By that, I mean understanding and accepting the fact that family business issues will occur, are normal, and will change as the business grows and as the family grows and ages;

2. Your PERSPECTIVE—Your way of thinking about family business issues taking into account the different perspectives of different people;

3. Your PROCESS—The structure and rules you adopt to proactively and preemptively manage family business issues; and

4. Your FAMILY VALUES—the values that you are seeking to teach and preserve and that should override personal rivalries, jealousies, and personal financial self-interest.

Our joint objective is simple:

DO *NOT* LET YOUR FAMILY DESTROY YOUR BUSINESS
and
DO *NOT* LET YOUR BUSINESS DESTROY YOUR FAMILY.

Just recently, I was being interviewed to be an advisor to a very successful fourth-generation Oklahoma family business with over 100 family shareholders. One of the board members asked me if my approach to family business issues had changed over the years. Yes, I answered. I have learned that:

1. You cannot manage family business issues in the same style or manner as most entrepreneurs manage their business;

2. The process or how family members have input, communicate, debate, and reach consensus is as important as the particular family issue or its specific resolution;

3. Family business issues are complex and it takes time for people to get comfortable—time for people to understand other people's perspectives and time for people to reach consensus;

4. Proactive and preemptive management of family business issues is better than reactive management. Proactively dealing with upcoming issues can mitigate uneducated opinions, anger, jealousies, and greed;

5. Values such as respect, integrity, fairness, love, and stewardship are the foundation of reaching results that are in the best long-term interests of both the business and the family; and

6. Caring, respectful listening is more important than a quick answer or a quick solution. In most cases, there are deeper family issues that need to be addressed, considered, and factored into the equation.

Let's begin our journey.

NOTE

1. J. H. Astrachan and M. C. Shanker, "Family Businesses Contributing to the U.S. Economy: A Closer Look," *Family Business Review* (September 2003): 218.

Chapter 1

Dynamic and Different Perspectives

As you learned in the Introduction, the family and the business are two overlapping interacting constantly changing organisms. Managing a family business is more challenging and is harder than managing a non-family business because of the family dynamics.

So starting off, one must accept the fact that family businesses are usually more complicated because of the added family dynamic. Your attitude, view, and openness to the following three key points are critical:

1. Family businesses have more issues than non-family businesses;
2. Family businesses are more complicated because of family dynamics; and
3. Family business issues are common, reoccurring, and predictable.

What is critical is the manner in which or how the Family Business Leader ("FBL")—the chairman-CEO of the family business—reacts to family business issues. Is he or she open, receptive, understanding, and accepting of family business issues or does he or she view them as a nuisance, hindrance, or irritant?

In working with family businesses, one of my first tasks is to advise FBLs that family business issues generally do not go away—they do not evaporate. Aggrieved family members do not go away nor forget their issues. Secondly, family members do not want their issues dismissed or handled in a summary manner.

The roles, job responsibilities, and duties of an FBL are not only to lead and manage the family business for business success but also to lead and manage the family's relationship to the business for family harmony.

Once the leader, founder, or family CEO of a family business acquires or adopts the right attitude or mindset about the added complexity of a family business, the normalcy of family business issues, and the need to deal directly with family business issues, the likelihood of continued business success and family harmony is increased. Why are there commonly occurring family business issues? What causes them to arise? And why are these occurrences predictable?

Most family business issues arise because of individual family members' psychological and financial needs. The human need for recognition, love, respect, to feel important, and to be valued all play a role as family members age. Likewise, as family members age, their financial needs change and they can view the family business as a means to meet those financial needs.

Once family members reach adulthood, marry, and have children, their views of the family business may change. All of a sudden, it may become more important to them because it represents an avenue or way to satisfy self-worth and financial needs.

Likewise, if some siblings or cousins work in the business and some do not work in the business, questions of favoritism and equitable treatment may arise, creating rivalries and jealousies if not handled properly.

If some family shareholders work in the business, those not working in the business may ask what benefits they are receiving from the business. If some family members are working in the business, all family members may want to work in the business.

How family members view the family business and what they may expect from the family business will change as their individual life situation changes. FBLs need to be sensitive and anticipate this as family members age. Every major life event . . .

- Reaching age 18
- Going to college
- Marriage
- Having children
- Buying a house
- Divorce
- Sickness
- Financial setbacks
- Private school or education costs for children
- Losing a job
- Reaching age 30, 40, 50, 60, 70 . . .
- Retirement
- Disability
- Death

... impacts family members, their needs, and how they view a family business. As an example, family members owning stock in a family business may not be concerned about cash dividends until they finish college or get married. Once they have more financial needs and pressures and want more income, the family business can be a source of that income. Family members owning stock in the business may not care about restrictions on the sale of stock or stock valuation issues until they need cash for private school or college. Family members not working in the business may not be concerned about the fairness or equity of other family members working in the business and receiving substantive salaries, benefits, and perks until they have financial pressures or increased needs.

You, as the family business leader, may not be concerned if the spouses of your children own stock in your business until there is a divorce. Then, do you want ex-spouses owning stock and coming to family business meetings? Likewise, as family members age and reach 40, 50, 60, or retirement age, their financial needs may increase because of sickness, disability, and the failure to save.

Any of these life events, almost all of which will occur to some family member, will change family members' psychological and/or financial needs and this will likely change their perspective of the family business. In most cases, these changes will increase the pressure for more dividends, more perks, more pay, and more stock liquidity.

Family business issues generally arise because family members want more from the business—not less.

Not only must you as the FBL be open, sensitive, and accepting of the fact that these life changes can create issues evolving around the family business, but also you, as the FBL, must be aware that these issues are more complex than the normal business issues of strategy, marketing, accounting, and finance because you are emotionally involved in and with the family and you have biases and preconceptions about your children, how they should act, how they should treat you, and how you should treat them.

In most cases, the affected person is your child, your niece, or your grandchild and is either an employee, a stockholder, or feels aggrieved because he or she is not an employee or shareholder while other family members are. It is these emotional components inside of you and inside of them that demand sensitivity and management skills and styles different than those commonly used in managing a business.

These emotional attachments make it difficult for many family members to be as direct, open, and honest with each other because people do not want to hurt fellow family members' feelings and because people like stability and harmony, not disagreement or strife.

If the family business is multi-generational or involves siblings or cousins and their families, then it is even more complex and fraught with emotional issues because not only do you have the feelings of the affected family member but you have the emotions and feelings of that persons' parents or siblings.

In many cases, FBLs are entrepreneurs—business builders. Entrepreneurs usually are people who are consumed and driven for success. They are confident, strong-willed, dominant personalities used to overcoming obstacles and problems through perseverance, willpower, and focus. Many have built successful business doing it their way. Entrepreneurs care about results—now! Entrepreneurs are comfortable with making fast decisions and moving on. Some entrepreneurs live by the management philosophy of "my way or the highway."

Is this familiar to you? Generally speaking, none of those usual entrepreneurial ways of acting will work well in resolving family business issues. Yes, out of a position of power or the control of the money you can coerce family compliance, but you cannot coerce or dictate family harmony. You cannot send the family "down the highway"—you have family, the good and the bad, for life. The family goes home with you at night.

A different management perspective or style is needed to manage family business issues. First, every family business issue should be viewed from two perspectives:

- What is best for the business?
- What is best for the family?

Secondly, a different management process and style is needed to manage the family side of the business. In managing family business issues, FBLs must:

- Be sensitive and emotionally intelligent;
- Be open and listen with respect;
- Be patient and respectful with those family members with less business experience;
- Try to listen, educate, and build consensus;
- Act in accordance with and teach family members the value of stewardship.

Dealing with family issues takes time—time to listen, time to think, time to educate, time to talk, and time to reach a consensus. How family issues are dealt with and how they are handled is as important as the resolution. To repeat: every issue should be approached from two perspectives with a sensitive, caring management style:

Table 1.1
Family Management Attributes

Negative Family Management Attributes	Positive Family Management Attributes
Rigidity	Flexibility
Impatience	Patience
Father-knows-best attitude	Listening
Controlling people	Respecting people
Fast decision process	Taking the time to listen and to educate
Command and control attitude	Empathy
Hierarchical or patriarchal attitude	Sensitivity
Lack of empathy	A caring manner
Lack of sensitivity	

- What is in the best interest of the business?
- What is in the best interest of the family?

Some examples:

Family business "A" had been very successful. It was owned by ten family members representing two branches of a family and two generations. It historically paid dividends to all shareholders since some did not work in the business. Family members were restricted from selling their stock except to other family members at an agreed upon valuation formula that takes into account the lack of marketability and liquidity and the minority interest. The founding generation was getting elderly and was concerned about management succession and their retirement security.

The younger generation wanted their turn to operate the business and had increasing financial needs because of larger, more expensive homes and the cost of private schooling for their children.

The company had strong competitors and management was concerned about the consolidation of the industry in which they operated and resulting downward pricing and profit pressures. Management was concerned whether a family business could survive in this hyper competitive environment.

The opportunity had arisen to buy a competitor. This competitor had a good management team and would both expand the product base and the geographical base of the business. But the sellers did not want to own stock in a family business; they wanted cash. The family business would have to finance the acquisition by taking on significant debt and would have to allocate almost all free and clear operating cash flow to finance the acquisition over the next seven years.

This is a classic case. You have two different generations at different stages of their lives with different financial needs. Put yourself into the "shoes" of the elder generation—what would their concerns be? How about the younger generation? What are their concerns? How about the concerns about the business's long-term viability?

In thinking about these different perspectives, not only should you think about financial concerns but also about personal job concerns of family members. How will the acquired management team fit into the family business management structure? Will the acquisition limit future employment or leadership opportunities for family members?

This case illustrates the potential conflicts between generations and the commonly occurring issue of the family business's capital needs conflicting with the family's need for more current cash.

Different perspectives will exist and have to be aired honestly, discussed openly, and even debated. The act of being sensitive to, acknowledging, and leading an all-encompassing family discussion about these different viewpoints is the act and skill of family business leadership.

It is the skills of sensitivity, empathy, listening, bringing out different viewpoints, building consensus, and ultimately making the hard decision— what is right for both the family and the business at this point in time and under these known circumstances.

Unfortunately, many FBLs make one of two common mistakes when facing difficult family business issues. The two most common mistakes are:

1. *Avoidance*—An attempt to avoid, delay, or hope family business issues will go away; and/or
2. *Denial*—the failure to accept reality or the facts generally concerning either their own limitations or mortality, or concerning the abilities of children.

Both of those common mistakes are rooted or based in human nature. People gravitate toward stability or the biological state of homeostasis. Generally, people do not like conflict or family emotional discomfort.

Normal first reactions of family business leaders who are facing difficult family business issues are:

- *Delay*—Now is not the right time to address the issue;
- *Avoidance*—The "aggrieved" family member will calm down after a while;
- *Avoidance*—Let's buy our way out of the issue by raising dividends and make him or her happy; or

- *Denial*—The "aggrieved" family member is either too young, or does not understand the business and his or her concerns are not justified.

My experience over 25 years is that family business issues do not go away. Rather, they fester and the aggrieved party or parties becomes more entrenched and angry not only about the issue but also about how he or she is being treated.

Being ignored or dismissed makes a family member feel like a second class citizen—not respected, valued, or cared about. Those feelings get exacerbated if the aggrieved party receives minimal economic benefits from the family business while other family members receive significant current economic benefits.

I have seen "avoided" problems boil over with lawyers being hired and then the consequences can range from estrangement to the forced sale of the business. Yes, it is easy in the short-run to try to avoid family business issues but these are the questions I try to focus my clients on:

"What are the downside risks of avoidance?"

"Is the emotional pain, costs, and consequences of the potential downside of avoidance greater than the discomfort of dealing with the issue now?"

Family business issues usually involve money. But beneath the actual money issues are usually emotional issues of intergenerational or intragenerational equity or psychological needs of wanting to be valued, respected, and loved by one's family. It is hard to face family business issues because you are dealing with family—people you care about (or should care about). Family does not get left behind at the office. Family is at home, at your dinner table, and in your bed. Family business issues cannot be avoided. And if they are avoided, they are avoided at a potential high peril and cost.

The second major and common mistake made by family business leaders is denial—the inability to face reality and facts. And when does denial usually occur? Denial usually occurs when a family business leader has to make decisions about either his or her competence or retirement or about his or her children and their competence and ability to work or lead the business. This commonly occurs when:

- An aging family business leader is no longer the best qualified person to lead the business;
- An aging family business leader is unwilling to give up control and power over the company;
- A male family business leader is unwilling to consider qualified female family members for employment, for leadership positions, or for board of director membership;
- A family business leader wants to appoint an unqualified family member to a major leadership position;

- A family business leader is unwilling to hold family employees to acceptable standards of performance and behavior; or
- A family business leader does not want to have to choose between children or relatives for a key position.

Other examples of commonly occurring destructive denial of reality issues arise when:

- Children are hired and/or promoted, and/or paid in excess of their competencies;
- A non-qualified son is chosen as a successor over a more qualified sibling;
- A loving founder promises family members financial benefits greater than the business can afford;
- Lazy, spoiled children employees impact non-family employee morale;
- A younger second wife is given a role in the business ahead of more competent and qualified family members;
- One expects family members not working in the company to continue to be satisfied without receiving current financial benefits from the business; and
- A founder believes his children will never want to sell their stock.

Children and their qualifications, competencies, strengths, and weaknesses are a very big issue. The realistic assessment and evaluation of a child's abilities and performance impacts whether they should be hired, how much they should be paid, and whether they are a future family leader.

How can you as the family business leader check your reality? By seeking independent, objective advice, verification, and evaluation. This is hard to do. It is hard to find senior managers in the business who will tell the boss the ugly truth. But a lot of that depends on you—how you react to the truth, and whether you hold the input confidential and private. People will tell you the truth if they trust you—trust that you will not "shoot the messenger" and trust that you will keep it absolutely confidential. Sometimes the independent, objective advice can come from an independent director, lawyer, or accountant.

One of my large family business clients wanted to go public. A lot of money was at stake. The patriarch was a strong, dominating, self-made man. He had dropped out of high school when his dad died and he worked on the farm. He ultimately built a billion dollar business. Both his son and his daughter worked in the business. Neither was respected or well-liked by the employees. Neither was that good at what they did. The children had an attitude of entitlement evidenced by each parking their brand new Mercedes cars by the front door of the business every day and expecting their cars to be washed for them by other employees.

As part of the going public process, the Wall Street underwriter raised the issue of succession since my client was in his 60s and was chairman and CEO. Finally, my client said he wanted Junior to be the president and his successor.

This result was so bad that even without being asked for advice, my client's law firm, accounting firm, and investment banker all told him that his son was not ready to be president. I, as the family advisor, called my client and asked to visit with him one Friday afternoon around 5 P.M. in order to talk.

I met with my client and raised the issue of the lawyers and others' advice. Not surprisingly, he asked my advice. I knew him and asked him, "Do you want it straight and direct?" He, of course, having been challenged, told me "Yes!"

I said, "George, I know you love your children and your dream is to have them run this company. Someday, that might happen. But the issue is whether Junior is ready to be president now. Has he earned the respect and trust of the employees, senior management, customers, and financiers? Does he have the skills required to deal with Wall Street and institutional investors? I don't think he is ready. Now is not the right time. I think it is the wrong result for both Junior and for the company."

He had leaned back in his chair as I talked and we looked at each other eyeball to eyeball. When I was finished, he rocked forward, leaned over the desk toward me and said, "This meeting is over." Then he got up and left.

My client did make his son president and unfortunately, my client died within a year. Then, Junior was made chairman and CEO and ultimately was forced to sell the company at a huge financial family loss because of his mis-management.

Another war story. A different person—a different result. During the go-go financial years of the 1990s, one of my private family clients wanted to go public. The founder was in his 50s and quite successful. He was a former CPA and had made millions in the energy industry. He was a strong-willed entrepreneur. He wanted to go public because he thought he could create more wealth in his new business as a public company.

He called me and said he wanted to show me some of the things he was working on and offered to pick me up in his private jet to take me around for the day. On the flight, he raised the idea of going public and talked about what a great public company CEO he would make. He shared his dream of building a billion dollar company. Small town boy makes good.

He then asked my advice. I talked at length about what a public company CEO does and what skills or competencies were needed. Then I told him he would be very unhappy doing what a public company CEO has to do and that his personality was not suited for the public markets. I told him if he wanted to maximize his wealth, he should consider selling his company to a public company and to build another.

It is now ten years later and that client took my advice because he sat back and realistically assessed who he was, what he enjoyed doing and how he wanted to live. He sold his company plus built and sold two others and is now worth over $100,000,000.

Dealing realistically with yourself and your family members takes an openness and honesty that is hard but IT IS vital to doing what is in the best interest of the business and the best interest of the family.

These common delay or denial mechanisms often lead to a reactive family business leadership style and philosophy. Many family business leaders wait till the proverbial pot is boiling over before taking action and, in most cases, emotions are at such a high level by that time that it is difficult to have reasonable discussions about the different perspectives and take the time necessary to reach consensus. As a result, there is a rush to do something—a rush to judgment that may only be a band-aid. I call this unfortunate chain of events a reactive family business management style.

In contrast to this reactive management style, there is an alternative that is more likely to prevent family blowups and that is a proactive management style that takes into account the changing perspectives of individual family members as their circumstances change and that preempts major disputes through a proactive process.

An example. One of my southern clients was a second-generation company with 50 family members as shareholders. Most of the shareholders did not work in the business and most lived in a state other than the one where the family business operated. Most of these shareholders were approaching age 50–60. The company paid a minimal dividend—less than $200 per shareholder per year.

For years, these shareholders looked at the seven family members who worked in the business and who were being paid $200,000 a year each and asked, "What about me? We need either current cash or liquidity."

For over five years the CEO tried to avoid the issue. Money issues do not go away. Feelings of unfairness do not go away. Avoidance lasted until there was a threat of a lawsuit and this ultimately led to the sale of the family business. Could the issue have been resolved without selling the family business? Probably—if the problem was not avoided for such a long time.

Another example. An entrepreneur who was a brilliant financier built from scratch a company worth $300,000,000. This gentleman was vibrant, hyperactive, and a financial wizard. He and his wife were well-respected members of the Denver political, cultural, and civic hierarchy. They had only one child—a son who was nothing like his father. A nice "C" student—not a leader, not smart, not an entrepreneur. The father refused to face reality and made his son CEO of the company with the father becoming chairman. What happened? The business faltered and the father had to step in and be more hands-on. Did the father then face reality? Yes and no. He now could verbalize that he and his son were very different but he avoided the correct answer—his son should not be CEO. He decided that he would restructure the company so that he and his son would each have a distinct part of the business to run—each would be CEO of part of the business, creating major issues with partners and employees.

In the next chapter we will discuss how to put in place a proactive family business management process.

Chapter 2

A Proactive Family Business Management Process

So far we have discussed that the management of a family business involves not only managing the business but also managing the family issues impacting the business.

We have discussed that managing family issues is not a one-time event but rather as the family members age and their circumstances change, these changes will impact their views of and needs from the family business. As one of my long-time family business clients said, "You can never take family harmony for granted when money is involved."

The main purpose of a proactive family business management process is to preempt and prevent major family disputes that put the business at risk and disrupt family relations. Family business issues will arise, they will arise frequently, and they are predictable; so what should you as the FBL do to deal with these realities?

Experience has taught me that you need a process—mechanisms and rules through which family members can:

1. Be educated often about the family business and its financial capacity and needs;
2. Be heard frequently and raise questions, concerns, and issues;
3. Discuss openly and understand family business issues from different perspectives and viewpoints; and
4. Reach consensus on what is in the best interests of both the family and of the business.

Any process that you adopt should take into account the underlying needs of family members to be listened to in a respectful manner and to have their views considered irrespective of age, gender, or business experience.

Table 2.1
Process

Good Process:	Bad Process:
Inclusive	Exclusive
Information transparency	Need to know basis
Respectful	Hierarchal/patriarchal
Two-Way frequent communication	Once a year

Let's discuss each point. What do I mean by inclusive?

INCLUSIVE

Inclusive means that every adult family shareholder and adult family employee and their spouses should be included in the process. The purpose of the process is to educate and communicate with all family members impacted by or involved in the business. Excluding family members who do not work in the business or family members who live out of state creates a two-class system that will frustrate your purpose—to preempt major family disputes.

Common questions from clients initiating a process include:

- What about spouses of family members?
- At what age should children or beneficiaries of family trusts be included?

From my experience, whether to include spouses of family members is an easy question. The answer is YES. And even if the spouses are not shareholders, the answer is YES.

Why should you include spouses? First, you want to educate them so when they are having discussions at home you lessen the impact of ignorance or rumors on feelings, judgments, and opinions. Spouses are going to have input either directly by participating in the process or indirectly through pillow talk. Spouses can be a mitigating influence on sibling jealousies or rivalries if spouses are treated with respect, communicated with, and given the opportunity to be heard. In cases where spouses are excluded, spouses who are uneducated about the business and the family's values and priorities can be a major factor in pushing their family member spouse to seek more power, money, or prestige, which fuels family strife.

The most common issue, according to my experience, arising for female spouses is that they want their husbands to be treated fairly and with the respect they are due by the family. The measurement of fairness and respect in many cases is money. Spouses have a hard time understanding differences among siblings in salary, stock ownership, and rank-position status. Female spouses compare what their husband receives against what siblings or cousins receive. On the other hand, my experience is that male spouses of female family members have different issues. Male spouses are more likely to have strong needs to impress and earn the respect of family members and to show their wives they are smart and as knowledgeable as her brothers. Male spouses want to impress their in-laws. So being inclusive has some negatives that have to be managed, but the positives of inclusion far outweigh those negatives.

Why is inclusion a hard issue for FBLs? Many family business leaders are knowledgeable business people and many are men with little patience, tolerance, and understanding for uneducated, inexperienced, and different viewpoints, and gender biases may also be in play.

Inclusion only works to mitigate and preempt family disputes if the participants feel like they are given opportunities to be heard and that their input is respected and taken into consideration. Making major decisions and then seeking input frustrates the purpose of inclusion, as does limiting input to family members working in the business, limiting input to family members with business or finance degrees, and limiting input to approving annual meeting minutes and annual financials.

In many multi-generational family businesses stock ownership is held in trust for grandchildren or children. At what age should these beneficiaries be included in the process of education and communication? Clearly, when the trust beneficiaries reach the age of 18, they should be included in the process and afforded full education, input, and communication rights irrespective of the terms or powers of the trust agreement.

One of my clients has over 200 different family shareholders spanning four generations. Because of the financial success of the business and its investments, many trusts were established for estate planning purposes. They adopted the rule of 18 that I set forth above. But they went further and they allow any beneficiary aged 15–18 to participate in the process if they desire to do so. Why? They have learned that the more family members know about the business, the less likely that rumors or misunderstandings can create false opinions or prejudices and feelings of being treated unfairly.

So keep in mind the purposes of inclusion—to educate and to give people the opportunity to be heard.

INFORMATION TRANSPARENCY

Inclusion works only if family members (including spouses) are given information about the business including detailed operating financials.

That information should include all the details about any financial dealings between any family member and the business including salaries, benefits, perks, the purchase of company inventory, or the sale of services or products to the company. Transparency means open book. Every family member shareholder should never be surprised by either the occurrence of, amount of, or timing of a financial benefit received by any other family member from the business.

This is a hard issue for many FBLs. Why? Well, for at least two reasons. First, knowledge is power and family business leaders are concerned about the wrong people knowing or finding out about the business, and they are concerned about losing absolute, dictatorial, or patriarchal control. Secondly, many FBLs think giving detailed financial information to family members may be a waste of time because they are not knowledgeable about the business or its finances.

Process is not just giving people numbers or reports. Process is much more. Process has two purposes—education and two-way communication. Process is explaining, teaching, and answering questions that can be elementary or complex.

RESPECTFUL

An inclusive, open-book process will not have the positive effects if family members' views are not solicited and listened to with respect. People want to feel that their input and views are respected, valued, and considered by the family. These discussions should be conducted with rules of participation:

1. All views should be listened to with respect;
2. People should not interrupt or characterize input as either stupid, ill-informed, or immature;
3. Views should not be critiqued in a personally offensive manner; and
4. Disagreeing or dissenting views should be encouraged.

The FBL has to set the tone and enforce the rules. He or she by his or her tones, words, and mannerisms should encourage openness, respect, and good discussion.

In many cases, family disputes can be prevented by these simple facts: give people the opportunity to have input into what they are a part of in a respectful and caring manner. Simple in principle, but so hard for so many entrepreneurs, business builders, and family leaders to execute. As in many business principles, the concept is easy. It is the execution—the doing—that is hard. Execution takes commitment, discipline, focus, and an iterative improvement attitude.

TWO-WAY FREQUENT COMMUNICATION

Managing the family side of the business takes time and effort and it is harder than managing the business because of the emotional relationships. Managing the family is work and sometimes it is not fun, but it cannot be avoided if you want to build or create a legacy business that survives one generation.

Many FBL clients of mine find it easy to buy in to the concept of process and the need for process and many have the immediate reaction that "okay, we will do this stuff every year at the annual meeting." As the family grows, once a year opportunities to ask questions or to be heard is not enough, in my judgment.

The process should include more frequent communications from the FBL to the family. The family members should frequently have a way to ask questions and give input. How can this be done?

Some of my clients invite any interested family member to attend any board meeting. One of my clients does a quarterly conference call with an 800 dial-in number for any interested family member. Another client holds its board meetings in different cities where family shareholders live. Others solicit questions and respond in writing to all shareholders—irrespective of whether they asked the question. Others adopt committee structures and populate the committees with family members not involved in the business on a daily basis.

There are many ways to give family members the opportunity to be heard and to have input but what is important is that the FBL's actions are consistent with his or her words. "Walk the talk" is so important in this area. As I tell my clients, the process is more important in most cases than the ultimate answer. If people and their views are treated with respect and dignity, they know that their view will not be adopted all the time—human nature is that people want to feel valued and feel a part of the family business.

Yes, some family members will want more power, more money and will have strong self-interests. But these tendencies can be better managed in an open, transparent process since "non-offending" family members will seek to uphold family stewardship values—what is best for the business and what is best for the family.

What are the components of a good proactive family management process?

1. Quarterly two-way communications to shareholders discussing business issues, financial results and upcoming family issues;
2. Quarterly board meetings with open attendance;
3. Annual audited financial statements distributed to all shareholders with question and answer sessions;

4. Annual family and shareholder meetings where education and input are emphasized—not the normal two hour meeting approving board elections, financials, and previous minutes of meetings;

5. The adoption and use of a Family Values Statement;

6. The adoption and use of a Family Code of Conduct;

7. The adoption of consistently applied Family Business Operating Rules concerning family employment, compensation, dividends, stock ownership, stock buy-back plan, and stock transfer rights.

The larger the number of family shareholders, the more geographically dispersed family shareholders are and the more generations involved, the more important a good institutionalized process will be. An institutionalized process is a consistently, frequently, and fairly applied collection of acts.

Putting it another way, process establishes the rules of the game amongst family members and it establishes the when, where, and how of raising and discussing family issues. Process is itself an education process and a two-way communication process and is intended to lessen family misunderstandings, rivalries, jealousies, and actions motivated by extreme self-interest. How family members are treated is important. The process of education and two-way communication is as important as the answer or result.

This process is the HOW of building family trust and the family's commitment to the fundamental principle that what is in the best interests of the family and of the business outweighs, or is more important than, the financial self-interest of any one family member.

So, how do you start the process?

Of course, your process has to be tailored to fit your facts and your needs. Key factors are the number of shareholders, the number of generations involved, and the geographical location—degree or amount of geographical dispersion of family members. My experience has been that the larger the number of family member shareholders and the more geographical dispersion, the more process you need in order to manage and preempt disruptive family issues.

The menu or cafeteria line of alternatives for a family business process include:

1. Adopt a Family Values Statement;

2. Adopt a Family Code of Conduct;

3. Adopt Family Business Operating Policies;

4. Quarterly written communications including detailed financial results to all shareholders;

5. Annual family meetings;

6. Annual audited financial statements distributed to all shareholders;
7. Quarterly board meetings open to all shareholders;
8. Quarterly informational conference calls for all interested shareholders;
9. Formation of family committees focusing on specific issues such as dividend policies, stock buy-back policies, family education, and family community service; and
10. The Board of Directors structured to represent different generations and branches of the family.

Many FBLs debate whether they should start a formal process now or wait until they have an issue or problem. As one FBL asked me, "Why wake a sleeping dog?" Another issue involved in creating a process is one of time. Many FBLs either do not have the time or want to make this a priority.

First, you as the FBL have to believe in the necessity of the process—that educating and engaging in open, two-way communications with family shareholders will increase the probability that the business will stay successful, be a legacy business, provide financial security for many people, and that the family will more likely remain harmonious relative to the business.

Or, allow me to state my point another way:

Unless you as the FBL believe in, support, and actively lead the creation, implementation and frequent execution of a family process, it will not be beneficial.

So, let us assume that you, as the FBL, are in agreement—that you are committed to family shareholder education, communication, and involvement. Now, what?

STEP I

To start with, I would call a family meeting and explain why you want to begin adopting a formal process and seek shareholder input. By having a discussion and seeking input as to what it is that the family members want or need, you are de facto engaging in the type of two-way involved communication so necessary for family engagement. Some of the steps you can take are easy—such as holding quarterly board meetings, having quarterly communications, preparing annual audited financial statements, and holding annual family meetings.

However, certain steps such as creating a Family Values Statement, a Family Code of Conduct, Family Business Operating Rules, or restructuring the board will take some time (6–12 months) because they in themselves are mini-processes that will take many discussions with all shareholders in order to generate educated, involved consensus.

The foundation and first building block for the more successful management of family issues is your Family Values Statement. It represents what your family stands for. Or, as one of my smarter clients called it, the "Family Brand." So chunk the work needed to be done in a logical order of steps to be accomplished and start one chunk at a time. Do not attempt to do too much too fast.

Most family business issues involve money and fairness. Frequently occurring conflicts include:

- Shareholders' desire for more cash dividends versus the business's need for working and growth capital;
- Individual financial self-interest versus stewardship—the good of the family and the business;
- Financial fairness amongst family members working in the business;
- Financial fairness between family members working in the business and those not working in the business; and
- Financial fairness between sons and daughters.

All of these types of issues should be discussed as part of the education process amongst shareholders. This sensitizes family members to what can happen and to commonly occurring issues that they will likely have to deal with.

As FBL, you should set the stage for why you think it is in the best interest of the family and of the business to create a process that will lessen the risk of family disputes as the business grows and as the family matures and grows.

The purpose is to put in place procedures to maximize family unity and business success. All family businesses face similar issues as they age and you want the family to be prepared for them and to have a way to resolve them. Business changes will occur. Family changes will occur. Differences of opinions will occur. All of this is normal and common. You need ways to deal with those changes and differences of opinion.

Your goals are good—you want the business to grow into something meaningful for the family and the family to be able to continue its success if that is what everyone wants. And what the family has to do is hard—to learn to listen to each other, to play fair, to respect different opinions—because as they age, they will be coming from different places and perspectives. Lay out a framework. First, we will create a Family Values Statement and then a Family Code of Conduct. Then we will discuss the make-up of the Board of Directors and Annual Family Meetings. Lastly, we will discuss creating Family Business Operating Rules.

I would recommend that you spend the first year creating the Family Values Statement, The Family Code of Conduct, and creating a representative board structure. At the First Annual Family Meeting, you should formally have all shareholders vote and approve the Family Values Statement, the Family Code of Conduct, and the Board of Directors structure. At that Annual Family Meeting, you should discuss prioritizing what Family Business Rules you need and the first priority will probably be stock ownership and transfer restrictions.

Your role as the FBL is to show you believe through your actions that:

- Every shareholder is entitled to their own considered viewpoint;
- Every shareholder is entitled to have that viewpoint listened to and responded to in a dignified and respectful manner;
- Each family shareholder has a duty to each other to try to reach agreement as to what is in the family's best interests;
- Different opinions are to be expected and we, together, will have to make some hard decisions; and
- We have to come to those decisions in a manner that we can be proud of.

Talk about the five common issues faced by all family businesses:

1. The conflict between shareholders' current cash needs and the business's need for capital;
2. The conflict between an individual's financial self-interest and stewardship—what is in the best long-term interests of the family and the business as a whole;
3. Financial fairness amongst family members working in the business;
4. Financial fairness between family members working in the business and those not working in the business; and
5. Financial fairness between generations.

The reason I recommend that you start the process with values is that the focus is not on money or on what people want from the business. I recommend that you begin at a higher level of thinking—something more meaningful, honorable, and lasting than greed. Most families I have worked with are surprised at how hard it is to create a Values Statement.

STEP 2

Once you have created an agreed-upon Family Values Statement, then you should move to a Code of Conduct. Many families question the need for formalizing a Code of Conduct, but I have found it to be a useful exercise with a result that can be used as an educational tool for children who will become shareholders or employees. Some obvious questions concerning getting the process started are:

1. Should all shareholders be invited and encouraged to participate? YES.

2. Should shareholders' spouses be invited to attend and participate? YES.

3. Should younger shareholders be invited to attend and participate? YES.

4. Should shareholders not working in the business and who have no business experience or knowledge be invited to attend and participate? YES.

Why? Let us remember our goals:

• Inclusion;
• Education;
• Two-way communications; and
• The preemption of major disputes

The hardest inclusion issue for some of my clients has been the spouse issue. Some families want to limit family members to direct descendants. Other families have a broader definition of family—both those born into it and those who marry into it. Remembering our goal is to proactively and preemptively manage family issues that will occur as family members age, my advice is to include spouses in your education and communication process.

Why?

My experience is that in-laws will play a major role in any major family business issue either directly or indirectly through their spouses. If that is the case, it is far better to have educated and informed input than uneducated and uninformed input. Although these are generalizations, here are commonly occurring in-law issues:

Daughters-in-law generally are concerned about whether their husbands are being treated fairly in comparison to siblings or cousins and whether they are getting the recognition, respect, and opportunity they are due from other family members. They are always comparing—comparing how much their husbands are paid to other family members' pay. Daughters-in-law can push their husbands to "stand up for themselves."

Nonetheless, participation of daughters-in-law can be very helpful. In one family dispute, it was the daughters-in-law that brought reasoned judgment to the table because they really identified with The Family Values. Likewise, I have had instances where the daughter-in-law saw her husband's lack of emotional intelligence and maturity and his lack of qualifications to be the successor CEO more clearly than her husband and advised him in the privacy of their home not to dispute the board's succession plan.

Sons-in-law generally act differently because their focus is different. They are less concerned with what their wife is getting financially but are more concerned with earning the respect of family members. They generally want to show everybody that they are smart. As a consequence, sons-in-law want to talk a lot and can take strong positions. Sons-in-law also try to coach and influence their wife's behavior and positions on issues.

So my rules of thumb are:

- When in doubt: include
- When in doubt: educate
- More communication is better than less

Managing a family process like this takes emotional intelligence and diplomacy skills. It takes time, effort, and hard work, all of which are justified by the goals of: increasing the probability that the family business will continue to be successful and increasing the probability that there will not be major family disputes. Remember our goal:

DO *NOT* LET YOUR FAMILY DESTROY YOUR BUSINESS
and
DO *NOT* LET YOUR BUSINESS DESTROY YOUR FAMILY.

Chapter 3

A Family Values Statement

The creation of a Family Values Statement can be a wonderful experience for all involved. What is important to your family? What is the relative importance of family harmony? Which is more important—the family or the business? What does family mean to a family member? What values should guide family behavior? What do we want the family to stand for? What should the family name represent in the community?

Family Values should be the foundation, the bedrock, the basic building blocks upon which family decisions are made. Family policies about, for example, dividends may change over the years, but family values should never change. They should be inviolate—yes, cast in stone.

All family businesses will face difficult and hard decisions regarding the allocation of financial results amongst family members, the roles and opportunities afforded family members in the business, the equitable treatment of family members not working in the business, and succession. In those difficult times, in the heat of the debate, family values are the underlying principles to be applied, principles to govern conduct—how the difficult issues are dealt with and the why certain results should occur.

The creation of a Family Values Statement forces the family to think about various scenarios and potential situations that can lead to family disputes and to discuss beforehand what the important values to be followed and applied are in those situations.

Discussing hypothetical, difficult scenarios involving potential family disagreements is a good way to educate and sensitize people to what may occur in a non-emotional, hypothetical manner. It is easy for a family member to say, "Remember when we discussed this when doing the Family Values Statement? Remember what we said?"

The most difficult value conflict for most families relative to the family business is prioritizing or ranking the importance of the family relative to the importance of the business. In difficult decisions that should have a higher priority—family harmony or the business? Some families decide that the well-being of the business overrides family unity because the business is the financial provider and security for many family members. And so what is best for the business is best for the family. This is what I call "The Golden Goose" principle.

Other families find it hard to adopt or conceptualize a hard and fast rule but rather take into account both family interests and the best interests of the business on a case by case basis depending on the facts and circumstances. Other families view the business as primarily a vehicle to provide for the family financially and thus, for example, policies of employment and compensation are not made on an arms-length business basis but rather on the basis of family needs.

In this latter case, I have had clients who adopted this view and, for example, have had five family members as senior vice presidents, all earning $150,000 annual salaries, all working six-hour days. In this case, it worked for those five family members until family shareholders not working in the business demanded their fair and equitable financial share.

Every family business is a unique combination of people, history, emotional relationships, needs, and experiences. Deciding what you want your family to stand for or represent and what you want your family business to stand for and represent is a defining step for your family business culture and your proactive family business education and communication process.

In creating and adopting a Family Values Statement, most of my clients have found this process to be much harder than they thought it would be and to take much more time than initially allocated. Why? Because words have different meanings for different people and drilling down from words to behaviors is hard for people. By focusing on what the meanings of certain words are, each individual is forced to participate in the creation of the Family Values Statement. They are forced to spend time thinking, analyzing, and coming to grip with these personal values and what is important to him or her individually.

Since different people will have different rankings of importance of values and different meanings in coming to agreed-upon or consensus values, the process involves a lot of discussion and open communication, and it takes time for people to reach consensus.

Family values are vital and the most important limit or restraint on individual greed and individual financial self-interest. Family values are important in dealing with inter- and intra-generational issues. Family values

FAMILY   HOW FAMILY
VALUES   ACTS

Figure 3.1. Values Are the Driver

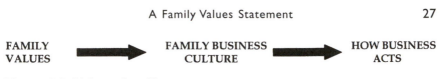

FAMILY VALUES → FAMILY BUSINESS CULTURE → HOW BUSINESS ACTS

Figure 3.2. Values Are Key

are determinative when dealing with the conflict of short-term benefits versus what is in the best interests of the business and family long-term.

During one stage of my life, I had the good fortune to work for one of the Bass Brothers of Fort Worth, Texas. In the 1980s and 1990s the Bass Brothers were one of the premier and legendary family investment groups. The man I worked for directly was David Bonderman, now the chairman of Texas Pacific Partners, one of the major international private equity firms. David was one of the most honest, direct, and brightest business people I have ever met or worked with.

Let me share with you a family values example that deeply affected me. We had a difficult business issue involving millions of dollars. There were legal questions and questions of what was right even if not legally required. We were having a debate about what to do when into the meeting walked Bob Bass himself. He came into the room quietly and went over to a corner and just listened. As we continued debating the issue, some in the room kept focusing on the legal documents that did not technically require us to pay. As we debated, Mr. Bass raised his hand and asked to speak. Here is what he said to us:

> **"Boys, you do what is right, no matter what it costs me."**
> Robert M. Bass, 1986

That, ladies and gentlemen, is family values in action. What message did he send to all of us? What did he want his family and his business to stand for?

What he said was that doing right was more important than money. And doing right may not be legally required. And in this case, it did cost him a lot of money. He told us what he represented, what his name stood for, and how he wanted his family business conducted. He said to do what is right even if it is not legally required.

Another way to think about this is something I learned from reading one of Bob Buford's books, *Significance—Not Success*. Visualize a large family tombstone in your town with your family name on it. This tombstone has room for only one word—that describes what your family stood for. What do you want it to say? Why did it matter that any of you were alive?

I have participated in many family meetings where there were genuine disagreements on what course of action to take. On several occasions, I have heard a family member say, "What would Grandpa have done?" or "What would Dad have done?" or "What would Mom want us to do in this case?"

I recommend that you do the work and adopt a Family Values Statement because I believe it helps families remain focused on what is important. It can be used as a guidepost or like a lighthouse beacon in tough times and it can be used to quell or mitigate jealousies, rivalries, and destructive, selfish individual behavior.

Get the family together and begin the discussion. Start out by making a list of potential values and include words like loyalty, stewardship, integrity, love, honesty, respect, and dignity. Once you have made up a list, take the time to discuss what the words mean to different family members. Discuss meaning until there is a common consensus about what the word represents and then make a list of potential values and definitions. Now comes the hard part—hard because most people skip this step or hard because most people are offended by it—but a necessary step to bring values to the real world.

Ask family members to rank the agreed-upon values in order of importance and ask them to confidentially write a dollar number like $50,000 or $1 million beside each value that represents the amount of money it would take to induce one to sacrifice that value. This focuses the family on the key issue it will face repeatedly—at what dollar number will an individual sacrifice family values or unity or harmony for personal financial gain?

Coming out of this process should be a written Family Values Statement. Families that I have worked with have, for example, agreed upon some of the following values:

Family Values Statement

As shareholders of the Smith Family Business, and as Smith family members, we all agree to abide by these values and to live our personal and business lives in accordance with these values. We will promote these values in all our dealings, teach them to our children, and we understand that along with the wonderful benefits of being part of this Family comes many responsibilities—including the responsibility not to do anything in our personal or business life to harm the family's good name and reputation and the responsibility not to brag or exhibit our financial blessings in a showy, gaudy, or flaunting manner.

We value **STEWARDSHIP**—our duty to pass on to the next generation a better company able to provide more opportunity and financial gain to our employees and family.

We value **HONESTY** in all our business and family dealings.

We will treat our customers, employees and each other with **RESPECT** and **DIGNITY**.

We value the **GOLDEN RULE**.

We value **SERVICE** to our community and to each other.

We want to stand for **QUALITY** products and be a good corporate citizen.

We will be **LOYAL** to each other and we will be there for each other during tough times.

We value **SELF-SUFFICIENCY** and our responsibility to be able to take care of ourselves.

We value **COURAGE**—doing what is right when it is hard.

We respect each other's **INDIVIDUALITY** and right to **PRIVACY** in non-family business matters.

We will truly listen to each other and try to understand different viewpoints and we will be willing to compromise in order to preserve family harmony.

The purpose of our business is to help give meaning to our lives and to our employees' lives.

We will conduct ourselves and our business humbly and not boast or flaunt our financial success.

The best interest of the family and of the business outweighs the financial self-interest of any one individual.

All shareholders shall sign this Family Values Statement and such signature is your commitment to be bound by these values.

I was talking with one of my neighbors—a very successful entrepreneur who built a $40 million company. And we were talking about his business and the tough decisions he often has to make. And he described the role of values beautifully:

**"The business is my legacy, and how it does business will
be how people remember me."**
Mark Norris, Carbondale, Colorado, 2003

Chapter 4

A Family Code of Conduct

Every family business should have a Family Values Statement as the bedrock or foundation for future generations' involvement in the business. A Family Values Statement is like the Constitution of the United States—the overriding themes or ideas. A Family Code of Conduct is more like the Ten Commandments—dictates of what behavior by family members is acceptable and what is not. A Family Code of Conduct is also like debate rules or parliamentary rules of order. They set forth how the game is to be played.

A Family Code of Conduct becomes more necessary as the number of family shareholders grows, as the number of family members not involved in the business grows, and as more inter- and intra-generational conflicts become possible.

As family businesses mature and become successful, this success creates more opportunities for conflicts, such as:

- The conflict between an individual's financial self-interest and family harmony or equity;
- The allocation of wealth amongst different generations;
- The allocation of opportunity amongst siblings or cousins;
- The allocation of wealth between those working in the business and those family members not working in the business;
- The choice of a successor CEO;
- What to do with excess cash produced by the business; and
- The distribution of power, respect, and love represented by business position or moneys derived from the business.

All of the above issues can create conflict, heated debate, hurt feelings, emotional responses, and even major family disputes and break-ups.

One purpose of a Code of Conduct is to try to manage these differences so people will act and express themselves in a manner that allows different perspectives and views to be aired and debated in a fashion that is respectful, dignified, and less hurtful.

Almost all of my clients have responded enthusiastically to the need for a Family Values Statement. With respect to a Family Code of Conduct, some have been reluctant or hesitant to adopt one because they think they have raised their family correctly and they will not have conduct issues. Others have said, "Let us wait until we have a problem and then the family members will better see the need for one" and other FBLs have stated that they run a "tight ship" and these types of rules are not needed.

These initial reactions are understandable and again, depending on the size of the family involved with the business, I believe these FBLs are being shortsighted. They are missing a great family education opportunity and an opportunity to discuss potential issues before they arise in a more businesslike manner.

Do not forget, just as in the case of creating a Family Values Statement, the creation of a Family Code of Conduct is in and of itself a process that will bring the family together to discuss and debate how they will address serious family business issues that will arise and are predictable as the family ages and more family members are involved. This process is not only a great educational experience but it is an opportunity for teaching family members how to raise, debate, and build consensus on important issues. The process is as important as the result.

The following is a hypothetical Code of Conduct to stimulate your thinking.

Code of Conduct for
The Jones Family

We all, as members of the Jones Family, agree to conduct ourselves in a manner that earns the respect and trust of others and to that goal we agree as follows:

1. Being part of the Jones Family and Business requires all family members to act in accordance with the treasured family values of stewardship, respect, integrity, trustworthiness, and humbleness and further, requires that we treat each other, our employees, and our customers with the dignity and respect that each individual deserves.

2. We acknowledge the good fortune that we have had to be born into this family and that such good fortune must be continually earned by acting in responsible ways.

3. We will in our dealings with each other, respect each other as individuals, acknowledge our differences, and seek to truly listen to opposing views and consider them.

4. We agree that family harmony and fairness is more important than each individual's financial self-interest.

5. We will be loyal to each other and provide as much emotional and financial support to each other in times of need—accepting our own individual responsibility to do our best and to be self-sufficient.

6. We, as owners of the Jones Business, acknowledge that our customers and employees rely on us and we will not let family personal matters undermine our responsibility to them.

7. All family business issues will be raised, discussed, and resolved in accordance with these rules and our Values Statement.

8. Any family member wishing to raise a question or issue about the family business should:

    A. Communicate directly with the CEO or the chairman of the board;

    B. The CEO or the chairman of the board shall promptly respond as necessary;

    C. Depending on the issue, the CEO or the chairman of the board may bring the issue to the Board of Directors at its next regularly scheduled meeting or if he or she deems the issue more urgent, pressing or time sensitive, may call a special meeting of the Board of Directors to discuss the issue;

    D. Depending on the issue or question, the CEO or chairman may elect to communicate either immediately or in the next scheduled quarterly shareholders communication or at the next Annual Family Meeting to all shareholders concerning the issue; and

    E. In all cases, the CEO or chairman of the board will respond to the family member as soon as possible as to the course of action and with an answer, if possible.

9. In the alternative, any family member may raise an issue by requesting that the chairman of the board schedule the issue for discussion at the next regularly scheduled Board of Directors

meeting. In such cases, the family member raising the issue may attend the meeting and be heard.

10. Further, in the alternative, any family member may raise any question or issue at the Annual Family Meeting by requesting that the question or issue be included in the agenda for the meeting under Family Business Issues.

11. No matter how the question is raised, the FBL, CEO, or chairman shall have the duty to make sure the issue is discussed, debated, and resolved in a timely manner and communicate directly the course of action and response to the family member raising the question. And, if appropriate for education purposes and in accordance with full transparency, but respecting individual privacy, such content will be distributed to all family members.

12. Discussions of family issues in any and all forums will be conducted with the proper respect, courtesy, and decorum. Outbursts, yelling, ad hominem remarks, constant interruptions, refusals to listen, refusals to give equal time to all views will not be tolerated or condoned. The chairman of the board has the responsibility to maintain proper order and decorum.

13. All family business issues will be subject to a vote that will be recorded with the vote being counted as one share of stock ownership equals one vote.

14. Each family member shall act in their personal and business dealings as if their actions will be on the front page of their hometown newspaper tomorrow.

15. All family members will use their best efforts and good faith to resolve all issues amongst the family. If this is not possible, then the Board of Directors shall appoint a three-person panel of independent, objective advisors—people of experience, integrity, and disinterest in the financial result to arbitrate the dispute in accordance with the rules of the American Arbitration Association. Such findings shall be final, binding, and not appealable to any court of law or equity. It is the family's intent to resolve all family issues in private and not in a court of law. Agreeing to this provision shall be a condition precedent to the ownership of stock in the family business.

16. All family shareholders are entitled to quarterly business financial statements and to annual audited financial statements and to have the opportunity to review, question, and understand the family business, its operations, and its finances.

17. Discretion, humbleness, and moderation are guides for our personal conduct and we shall abstain from gaudy, ostentatious evidence of our family wealth or success.

18. Fairness, respect, dignity, and integrity shall be the guiding principles in all our discussions.

19. All family members agree that the best interests of the family require that issues be raised and aired in a proper manner and in a proper forum and that it is improper to create or to conspire to create family cliques, family factions, family coups, or family divisions.

20. All family members agree and understand that it is not possible for everyone's personal viewpoint, judgment, or opinion to be the resulting answer and that the FBL, the Board of Directors, and the shareholders have the duty to do what is in the best interests of the business and the family as a whole.

21. When in question, the Family Business Leader, the CEO, and the chairman of the Board of Directors should act to insure family involvement, family communication and input, and family stewardship in the raising and debating of all questions or issues raised by family members.

A Family Code of Conduct will not guarantee family harmony. But it can be a tool to moderate conduct and limit inappropriate, hurtful conduct or communications and emotional outbursts.

But unfortunately, in some cases, an individual family member may put his or her greed, ego, or needs above all else and create a hurtful, hostile situation. In such cases, the FBL, the CEO, the chairman of the board, and the family members should strongly stand for adhering to the Family Values Statement and Code of Conduct. Inappropriate behavior cannot be condoned or tolerated. Inappropriate behavior lowers the standards of conduct.

Let me share with you two examples of family disputes that I have witnessed.

In the first case, two brothers inherited from their father a small business that over 25 years the brothers built into a business worth over $100 million. The older brother was the quiet, reserved one who worked on the details of the business out of the public spotlight. The younger brother was the public persona of the business. The older brother had two sons working in the business and had hopes that one of them would run the business someday. The younger brother had two daughters not working in the business and one son-in-law working in the business who was very ambitious and desired to be the successor CEO.

As the brothers aged, neither would talk about the difficult issue of succession in an honest, open way and about the upcoming competition between the son-in-law and a son for the leadership position. As can be expected in these situations, the son and son-in-law engaged in competition and behavior to make themselves look better than the other and behavior to expose the other's mistakes and deficiencies.

This environment created family tensions and, as can be expected, wives and daughters got involved. This was a family business waiting to explode—all because of failed values and a flawed process.

A public explosion was avoided. But family harmony was destroyed in the resolution of the issue. The issue was resolved in a manner completely devoid of values or respect. It turned that out the older brother was having an affair with his secretary. The younger brother, upon finding this out, had the adulterous couple followed and photographed in compromising situations by a private detective. And the younger brother used these pictures to "blackmail" the older brother to sell his ownership position in the family business to the younger brother, thus resolving who would be the successor leader—the son-in-law.

Your first reaction is probably one of disbelief. But family members are people and sometimes people act in selfish, mean, and hurtful ways.

My second example could have ended as badly but for the wisdom, judgment, and values of the FBL. This family was a third generation family business with two sisters being the surviving matriarchs. The CEO/chairman was the husband of one of the matriarchs. The shareholders of the company were split 50/50 between the two branches of the family and family members from both branches worked in the business.

The oldest child of the two sisters was given a position of substantial authority and was the unofficial heir apparent CEO. However, over a period of time, that son acted in ways to earn the mistrust and disrespect of his cousins. In addition, this elder son started acting and talking like he was the chosen family leader successor. As you can imagine, this situation was ripe for a major family blowup. But as I have stated, the CEO/chairman was a wise man who, as the husband of one of the two matriarch sisters, understood that family unity and harmony was paramount and how this situation was to be handled was critical.

What did he do? The CEO/chairman knew this issue was alive and being discussed "behind closed doors" by family members. He knew that his children had strong feelings about the offending cousin. He knew he could not hurt his wife's sister. So he hired a consultant—an independent, objective advisor who met individually with every family member shareholder and with every spouse of every family member shareholder to discuss the succession issue.

The issue of the cousin's behavior was discussed in the context of who was the right person to lead the family business into the next generation.

The consultant framed the issue as first the family needed to define the attributes, values, and skills they wanted in a successor leader. It was this process of defining the qualities and competencies of leadership that allowed both sides of the family to reach unanimous consensus validating family values. The search for shareholder input on a confidential, individual basis from every shareholder and every spouse gave everyone the opportunity for open, honest, and direct input. The consultant's demeanor and method earned the trust of the whole family.

Not surprisingly, both sides of the family were in agreement that the elder son was not the right person to be the successor and they wanted the CEO/chairman to begin training a different family member for succession within five years. Even the elder son's wife did not want her husband to be the successor CEO because she knew that would create great family disharmony.

Ultimately, the only person favoring the elder son as CEO was the elder son. Unfortunately, he had a difficult time giving up his dream. As a result, the family decided to sell one division of the business to the elder son and he left to run that business. He was able to be a CEO outside the family business and family harmony and values were preserved.

It would be unfair for you to think that what this family did or went through was easy. It was not. It would be wrong to infer that this family reached these results quickly—results that were right for this particular family in their particular circumstance. They did not. It took over a year for the issue to be resolved.

But all during that time, family members kept their eyes on the goal of the right answer for the family and the business long-term. They conducted themselves in such a manner so as not to escalate emotions and in a manner that allowed everyone to maintain their dignity.

Chapter 5

Annual Family Meetings

The third structured element of creating a process by which family business issues can be raised is the Annual Family Meeting. Annual Family Meetings should be viewed as a tradition and as a way to bring all family members together for education, discussion, and proactive management of the family and the business.

Most family businesses hold an annual shareholder's meeting because it is required by state corporate law. Such annual meetings generally last two hours and include approving a slate of directors for the board, approving the annual financial statements, approving all acts of the board and officers during the past year, and a concise high level review of financial results.

This type of annual meeting may be appropriate in small family businesses where all of the shareholders work in the business and have detailed knowledge of the operations of the business. However, it is not, in my judgment, appropriate for family businesses with a meaningful number of family shareholders who are either multi-generational or not working in the business.

Annual Family Meetings are wonderful opportunities in those cases to:

1. Communicate and educate all family members—young and old, those not working in the business, and spouses—about the current state of the business and its challenges and opportunities;

2. Reaffirm family values and to teach them to younger members of the family and to spouses;

3. Discuss and anticipate future issues such as dividend pressures, stock liquidity needs, retirement, and succession;

4. Bring in outside experts to educate the family on issues of importance to the family; and

5. Celebrate the family and the business.

As the family business grows and expands its shareholder base and as family members move away from home, annual family meetings can bring everyone back together at a set time each year for a combination of business and family reasons.

One of my clients has about 25 family shareholders spanning three generations and two branches of the family. The younger generation has young kids so there is the fourth generation of cousins. The family has, over the years, become geographically dispersed. They hold their Annual Family Meeting on the second Friday in December every year and around the Family Meeting they have a family holiday weekend—a wonderful tradition.

Another of my clients has approximately 180 family shareholders spanning four generations. So, including young children, at least five generations are involved. This business holds its Annual Family Shareholder Meeting on odd years at the home base of the company over a two-day period. However, on even years it holds its annual meetings at an appropriate resort environment and all shareholders and all family members are invited for four days of meetings, recreation, and discussion about family and business matters.

Because that family business is facing issues of succession, retirement, and maintaining the emotional connectedness of younger generations not working in the business, they are considering having every Annual Meeting be a full family meeting.

More and more of my clients are viewing Annual Meetings as a time to teach family values, traditions, and basic business skills to younger family members and spouses. Multi-generational, wealthy family clients look at these Annual Meetings as an opportunity to teach responsibility, self-sufficiency values, and skills to those younger family members interested in starting a business.

Annual Family Meetings for some families are the one time of the year that everyone's input can be solicited while everyone is present and everyone can listen in person to different perspectives on various issues.

Annual Family Meetings should be structured to educate and to allow for questions and opportunities to be heard. They should not be something seen as obligatory or as a burden. They should also be fun—time to share and deepen ties.

Who should attend the business part of the Annual Family Meeting? All shareholders and their spouses and children above the age of 15, if they want to. Again, keep in mind your goals of inclusion, education, and communication.

Should there be time set aside in the Family Meeting Agenda for family members to ask their questions about the business, its operations, and its finances? YES, and those questions should be encouraged.

Bring in outside speakers and educate family members on economic issues, political issues, how to manage their lives better, how to read finan-

Table 5.1
Sample One-day Family Meeting Agenda

8:00–8:30 A.M.	Continental Breakfast
8:30–9:45 A.M.	CEO Presentation and Q&A Session on the "State of the Business," Industry Trends, Customers, Competitors, Opportunities, and Challenges
9:45–10:00 A.M.	Break
10:00–11:15 A.M.	CEO Presentation on Financial Operating Results with Q&A
11:15–Noon	Questions
Noon–1:15 P.M.	Lunch with Speaker—"Why Most Family Businesses Fail in Succession Planning"
1:15–3:00 P.M.	Shareholder Committee Reports A. Family Values Committee B. Dividend Policy Committee C. Charitable Contribution Committee D. Board of Directors Committee
3:00–3:15 P.M.	Break
3:15–5:00 P.M.	Discussion of existing upcoming potential family business issues
5:00 P.M.	Conclusion
6:00 P.M.	Dinner

cial statements, how to make investment decisions, how to compute rates of return, the impact of globalization on the business, outsourcing, how to use technology to increase efficiency and productivity, and the trade-offs of efficiency and employee loyalty and morale.

Think outside the box and consider outdoor team building exercises, improvisation theatre creativity exercises, diversity training, communication skills, or bring in the CEO of a non-profit or charity to discuss the problems of leadership. Use the Annual Meeting to educate and broaden the horizons of the family—like continuing education about different issues.

You will be surprised at the results. First, you will have good attendance. Second, you will keep family members living away from home or not working in the business more connected and involved in the business, and you will be continually communicating, educating, and emphasizing those areas that are important to you. It is worth the time, cost, and effort to make the Annual Family Meeting as informative and educational as possible.

Table 5.2
Sample Two-day Family Meeting Agenda

DAY ONE

8:00–8:30 A.M.	Continental Breakfast
8:30–9:45 A.M.	CEO Presentation and Q&A Session on the "State of the Business"
9:45–10:00 A.M.	Break
10:00–11:15 A.M.	CEO Presentation on Financial Operating Results with Q&A
11:15–Noon	Questions
Noon–1:30 P.M.	Lunch with Speaker
1:30–3:00 P.M.	Committee Meetings A. Family Values Committee B. Dividend Policy Committee C. Charitable Contribution Committee D. Board of Directors Committee
3:00–3:15 P.M.	Break
3:15–5:00 P.M.	Committee Reports and Discussion
6:00 P.M.	Dinner

DAY TWO

8:00–8:30 A.M.	Continental Breakfast
8:30–9:45 A.M.	Personal Financial Planning Session
9:45–10:00 A.M.	Break
10:00–11:15 A.M.	Personal Tax and Estate Planning Session
11:15–Noon	Questions
Noon–1:30 P.M.	Film from Stanford Business School
1:30–3:00 P.M.	Group Activities
3:00–3:15 P.M.	Break
3:15–5:00 P.M.	Dinner—Family Awards Speaker: _____

REVIEW SESSION

Let us stop for a minute and think about some of the key points that we have discussed in Chapters 1–5.

First, family businesses are living, changing organisms and are more complex and harder to manage than non-family businesses.

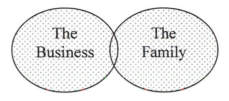

Figure 5.1. The Overlap

Most family businesses face similar issues as the business grows and matures and as the number of family shareholders grows.

As families age, expand, and grow in numbers and generations, family members' needs and viewpoints will change as their financial and emotional needs change.

The management of the family side of the business can be made easier by adopting processes that give family members the opportunity to be heard, to give input, and to be a part of deciding the destiny or fate of the family business. Family business shareholders need to be emotionally connected to the business.

Managing the family side of the business takes skills and competencies that many family business CEOs are not good at:

- Listening;
- Patience;
- Teaching;
- Empathy; and
- Emotional Intelligence

Hierarchical, patriarchal, dictatorial, top-down management styles will not work well with multi-generational family shareholders.

Because of the challenges of managing family issues, family business leaders often try to avoid dealing with family issues and, in some cases, hope they will disappear or dissipate on their own. Avoidance usually solves nothing.

Family businesses will have family issues. Whether it is issues of nepotism, equity amongst siblings, equity between different generations, financial equity between family members working in the business and those not working in the business, succession, stock liquidity, or older generations who will not let go—you will have issues and how you raise, discuss, and resolve family business issues is as important as the resolution in keeping family peace.

Families need rules of engagement and agreed-upon values that can help them through disputes or differences. Families need to teach and live by certain values such as integrity and stewardship.

Family members should be taught that the good of the family and of the business outweighs any one individual's financial interests.

A family business leader has an awesome responsibility: managing both the business and the family's involvement in the business.

A good family business leader accepts that responsibility, proactively manages both, and is constantly being a good CEO by:

- Communicating with the family and
- Educating family members
- Often.

Chapter 6

Employing, Compensating, and Managing Family Employees

As family businesses grow, it is every founder's hope that his or her children will work in the business and continue his or her legacy. This issue of legacy becomes complicated because the family must face the following issues:

- How many family members are qualified to work in the business?
- How many family members can the business afford to hire?
- Should family members be required to have prior work experience?
- On what basis should I hire family members? Merit? Nepotism? Need? Right?
- How should family members be compensated?
- How will family employees affect the performance and motivation of non-family employees?
- Who will manage family employees?

Most families go through stages in dealing with these issues. Very little thought is usually expended upon the hiring of the first family member and issues usually arise when there are a significant number of children, cousins, or grandchildren who view the family business as an employment opportunity or right.

Not surprisingly, the basis on which the first family members are hired sets expectations and precedents for future cases that, if not followed, leads to issues of favoritism and family members feeling as if they have not been treated fairly as compared to their brother, sister, or cousin.

These issues not only can impact the family dynamics but also the hiring of and conduct of family employees can impact the business culture and the motivation level and performance of non-family employees.

In thinking about the issues of hiring, compensating, and managing family employees, it is helpful to look at the issues from at least four different perspectives:

1. What is in the best interests of the business?
2. What is in the best interests of the potential family employee?
3. How will hiring a family employee impact the non-family employees?
4. What precedent, expectations, or issues will be created with future family members who may want to work in the family business?

As your family grows, ultimately you will need a family employment policy that is consistently and fairly applied. As you would imagine, as the number of family members and shareholders grow, the issues become more complex and pressing. Family members not working in the business will naturally ask:

"What am I getting out of the business?"

"Why does Cousin Jim or Cousin Jane get a high-paying job and I do not?"

"Why am I being treated differently?"

In coming to your own conclusions about whether, how many, on what basis, and at what compensation to hire family members, it is important to decide what you want the family business to do for the family. By that I mean, do you want the business to provide job opportunities for as many family members as possible, or do you want the business to operate like an independent business—creating wealth for the shareholders?

Is the family business first and foremost a business or should it be like a family club? Is the purpose of the family business to financially provide for as many family members as possible? Some additional points to think about:

1. The larger the number of family members working in the business, the more likely that there will be family rivalries, jealousies, and competition for pay, status, and leadership positions;
2. The larger the number of family members working in the business, the more important standards of conduct and performance become because it is very hard to run a business with two different standards of performance—one for family employees and one for non-family employees;
3. What is right for the individual family member?
4. What can the business afford? How many family employees can the business afford?

Ultimately, you will decide on an operating principle and you basically have two diametrically contrasting choices:

Arm's Length Market Rules
vs.
Favoritism for the Family

What many family business leaders fail to do is to think ahead and ask:

- Am I creating opportunities for family conflict?
- Am I increasing or decreasing the probability the business will be successful long-term?
- Am I sending the wrong messages to my non-family employees?

This is a critical issue because it can be the seed of two very potentially destructive feelings of inequity or unfairness:

1. The larger the number of family members working in the business, the more likely there will be rivalries and jealousies and competition regarding pay, position, and succession. Remember if you have three or four children and/or cousins working in the business, there is only one CEO position; and

2. If you have some family members working in the business receiving compensation, benefits, and perks and other family shareholders not working in the business, there can be intense feelings of unfairness and inequity, i.e., what does the non-working brother, sister, or cousin receive from the business?

The right answer for you will depend upon your particular facts and circumstances, but let me share with you my conclusions after seeing many families tussle or wrestle with these issues:

1. Every family member working in the business needs their own "space"—an opportunity to earn respect, recognition and to perform on their own;

2. It is hard for siblings or cousins to work for each other;

3. Parents are generally poor managers of children;

4. Family employees should be held to at least the same standard of conduct and performance as non-family employees; and

5. Hiring, compensating, and measuring family employee performance based on merit and market rates is far easier to implement on a fair, consistent basis than favoritism for family members on an ad hoc basis.

Over the years there are several questions that families have asked me repeatedly as they think through what is the right answer for them regarding family employment. Should family members wanting to work in the business be required to work a minimum number of years outside the family business before joining the family business?

Yes, I would encourage young family members to get some great training and work experience first outside the family business for several reasons. This will give them the opportunity to learn and perform in a more objective environment—increasing their self-confidence and credentials. Secondly, most family businesses do not have formal training programs like many large and even medium size business, and one's first job should maximize opportunities to learn. Thirdly, success in the "real" world carries over to the family business. Non-family employees will more likely respect the fact that the family member earned his or her way in a non-family business first and is due their respect and followership.

Another common question is to whom should the family member report to or work for? In the beginning, depending on the experience, age of the family members and the depth of senior management in the family business, it is usually better for the family member to report to and work for a senior, trusted, non-family employee who is a good teacher. Again, family members should want to earn the respect and trust of fellow employees and this is one way—perform accordingly to consistently applied high standards by a neutral boss.

What are the downsides to hiring family employees? Well, first, I have talked about the harmful potential effects on the individual family member if they are treated with favoritism and we have talked about sibling and cousin rivalries and competition for pay, leadership positions, etc. One further point: Family member employees can have a disruptive and devastating effect on a business's performance and employee morale if the family employee behaves in an arrogant manner or in a non-professional manner, flaunting rules, and/or treating employees with disrespect. Family business leaders cannot allow dysfunctional family behavior to be transferred into the business environment. Such would be destructive and could lower employee efficiency, productivity, morale, and respect for the family.

Okay, you have decided to hire a family member based on merit, qualifications, and you have weighed the potential downside of sibling or cousin rivalries, employee issues and whether this is good for the family member. How do you compensate the family member? Who performs his or her annual performance review?

It should not surprise you that family employee pay can become a BIG issue when you have many family shareholders, many of whom do not work in the family business. Family employee pay, perks, and benefits will be the subject of comparison and envy by non-working family shareholders. On what basis or how do you justify, defend, and diffuse these potential issues?

The only effective way to dispel the issues of favoritism and non-equitable treatment amongst family members is:

- Hire family members based on merit, qualifications, and needs;
- Compensate family members on an arms-length market rate basis for the particular job; and
- Evaluate, promote, and demote family employee performance based on consistent standards that are applied to all employees.

Even if you do this, some non-working family members will want to receive like financial benefits from the family business in some way or manner. These family members have to understand that the employed family member is doing a job—working for his or her pay and that the non-employed family member has the opportunity to earn market pay in the market place, too.

Not unexpectedly, if a family business employs a few family members and has many non-employed family shareholders, the non-employed shareholders will advocate the need for meaningful cash dividends as a way for them to receive some financial benefit from the company.

As your family grows and as you have some family members working in the business, I am frequently asked whether family salaries or benefits should be disclosed to all family shareholders.

Yes, because you want people to understand your policies of need, merit, and arm's-length market pay. And the facts being fully disclosed can engender understanding and overcome rumors and opinions formed without adequate information.

How should family employees' performance be reviewed? By whom? On what basis? How will promotions and raises be determined? On what basis will family members be terminated? Can they be rehired?

Family HR policies become, again, more important as the number of family members employed increases, especially in the cases where you have non-employed family shareholders. Again, let us use a perspectives approach.

From the perspective of the particular family employee, they are an individual with state and federal legal rights; and as importantly—feelings; most want to earn the trust and respect of their peers. They should want to be treated fairly and earn their way.

From the perspective of non-family employees, they will watch and judge management on how they treat, manage, and promote family members. Why is this important? Because if you have two standards it could undermine morale and it could create legal issues when you want or need to terminate a non-family employee.

Finally, from the perspective of other family shareholders, they have separate and distinct rights as minority shareholders. They want the business to pay market rates for market performance.

The most defensible policies are that family employees should be subject to the same HR policies, standards, reviews, and rules as non-family employees. The difficulty in this area is not in deciding the rule but rather in the implementation of the rule.

Can a parent fairly and objectively evaluate and critique on an arm's-length basis a son's or daughter's performance in a manner that is fair to all concerned? Can a brother evaluate and critique his brother's or sister's son or daughter?

No easy answers. Some families in larger businesses have other non-family senior managers perform annual reviews of family employees. Other family businesses have independent non-family board members review all family employee performance ratings.

Whatever method you adopt, you have to attempt to negate feelings of favoritism, feelings of double standards, and negatively impacting non-family employee morale and standards. This issue arises when children coming into the business were given too much as teenagers, were spoiled, or were not taught the value of hard work. Such children have an "entitlement" attitude and expect special treatment from the family business and non-family employees without paying their dues or earning the respect and trust of non-family employees. My experience is that second or third generation sons are the worst violators of these rules.

Bottom line—for the good of the family business and for the good of the individual family employee, for family harmony and equity amongst family employees and non-employed family shareholders, apply the same standards and rules to all employees fairly and consistently.

In order to get other managers to manage family employees willingly and honestly, you must not "kill the messenger." If you are going to fire a manager who holds your son's feet to the fire, you may as well manage your son yourself. If you are going to take your son's viewpoint and override his immediate supervisor, you may as well manage your son yourself.

If you are going to put in place a system whereby family members are held to the same standards as non-family employees, then for the good of your business you need to abide by the rules based on fairness and consistency.

Chapter 7

Corporate Perks, Benefits, and Dividends

Family businesses with family shareholders not working in the business all face the following recurring questions from those shareholders:

- "What do I receive from the business?"
- "What does the business do for me?"
- "What benefits do I receive by being a shareholder?"
- "What value does my stock really have?"

Other common issues are determining the line of demarcation between the business and family shareholders. Should family shareholders be able to ask employees to do shareholder's personal work or chores? Should family shareholders be able to come into the business and "take" inventory? Should the business reimburse family shareholders for country club dues? Should the business buy products or services from family shareholders? Can family shareholders use company trucks or cars? To whose (which family shareholders) favorite charities will the business make contributions?

The larger the number of family shareholders and the smaller the amount of annual cash dividends, the more important the issues of benefits and perks become. The first step in analyzing the issues of corporate perks and benefits is to come to some family consensus on what the business should represent to the family.

On the one hand, some families view the business as distinct from the family and its operation should be on an arm's-length basis subject to the business's paramount duties to its customers and its employees. I call this approach euphemistically the "public" company approach—although that terminology has been besmirched by the recent public company financial scandals.

The other approach is the "family piggy bank" approach that blurs the lines between family and business and treats the business as one big piggy bank from which the family makes withdrawals. One problem with this approach is that as the number of family shareholders grows, the number of potential withdrawers grows and the "piggy bank" only has so much money.

The second problem created by the "piggy bank" approach is the resulting compulsion of each family member to compare what he or she receives from the business to what others receive, and the need for fairness and consistency.

Is the family business separate and distinct from the family except for paying salaries and dividends? Or, is the family business and the family interchangeable? Most of my clients have adopted middle-of-the-road positions—that is, specific perks or benefits are allowed and other than those allowed perks or benefits, the family cannot use or avail itself of corporate assets or opportunities.

Some examples:

Family Business "A" consists of three generations of shareholders totaling 40 individuals. All shareholders receive life and medical insurance benefits and small annual dividends paid for by the business. The business does buy services on an arm's-length basis from two entities owned by sons-in-laws. And the family may use the corporate plane if they pay the operating costs. Lastly, the business prepares all the shareholders' individual federal and state tax returns.

Family Business "B" operates on an arm's-length basis like a public company. Shareholders receive only those benefits afforded to public company shareholders, i.e., dividends and directors fees, if applicable.

Family Business "C" allows family members to buy inventory at cost and to use corporate vehicles. The business also makes charitable contributions to favorite charities of family members.

Family Business "D" was owned by a brother and his sister. The business was divided into two operating divisions—one run by the brother and the other by the sister's husband, the brother-in-law. Each division operated separately in totally segregated offices on half of the top floor of an office building. Each division had a completely separate office suite including reception areas, conference rooms, offices, private dining rooms and kitchens. The corporate jet had two distinct and complete interiors and furnishings— one for each side of the family—separate carpet, linens, china, and chairs. This family applied the separate but equal theory.

Corporate dividends are a big issue in most family businesses, especially if you have a large number of shareholders not working in the business. Dividends may be the only financial or finite benefit of stock ownership for these family members as compared to those receiving compensation as employees.

Most families want the company to both keep growing and to pay large dividends. In most cases, the business cannot maximize both growth and pay large dividends. There is only so much free cash flow for investment and the payment of dividends. The "money pie" is only so big.

So there is constant tension between the business's need for growth capital and the family's need for larger dividends in order to keep non-employed family shareholders happy.

As we will see, this sometimes unrealistic pressure for large dividends can result in shareholders wanting liquidity options—all of which is caused by the previous transfer of stock to children and grandchildren in order to save estate taxes. The unintended consequences of this estate planning technique is to create stress and pressure first for dividends and ultimately for stock liquidity.

How do you deal with this issue of family shareholders wanting growth and dividends? My experience is that in most cases, family shareholders have never had the business's working capital and capital investment needs explained to them. In every such case I have been involved in, uninformed family shareholders have become realistic and reasonable when they understand the business's financial numbers showing free cash flow and its potential uses. In every case when they make educated and well-informed choices, they have chosen long-term investment over short-term personal greed.

The facts of most family businesses are:

1. The "money pie," that is the amount of money available for dividends or stock buy-back plans is only so big—it is finite;
2. Maximizing both business growth and shareholder dividends is not possible; and
3. When confronted with a choice, most shareholders vote for growth.

Nonetheless, dividends can be very helpful in managing family businesses with large numbers of shareholders who are geographically dispersed. In two cases, the payment of some dividends has kept family peace between those family members working in the business and those not. In another case, those dividends motivated younger shareholders to get involved in learning about the company, its values, and entrepreneurship. Lastly, if the family business brings in outside non-family management, dividends for family members become an important part of the scorecard—how the family grades the management team.

One of my clients has the patriarch of the family give each (50) shareholders his or her dividend check at the Annual Family Meeting. The amounts of the dividends range from $2,000–$10,000 per person and it has a big impact on family morale.

Again, as the number of family shareholders grows and as they become geographically dispersed, the pressures for either meaningful stock dividends or a stock buy-back plan will grow. If founding shareholders make annual gifts of family business stock to children and grandchildren, they will face these issues.

One of my clients was in business in the South and had 20 shareholders—17 of whom did not work in the business. The 3 working in the business each received on average $200,000 a year in pay and benefits. No dividends were paid and there was no stock liquidity program. Guess what? After years of ignoring family members' requests and outside independent advice, the 17 forced the 3 to sell the company—ending a three-generation family legacy because of insensitivity and poor family management.

There are two other commonly occurring issues:

- Should the family business make loans to family members?
- Should the family business buy products or services from family members?

The issue of family loans raises the question of to whom and for what purpose? Should the business make loans for home down payments, college educations, or medical emergencies? In many cases, most of the family's wealth is tied up in the business. Should a benefit of ownership be access to that safety net?

The most important, most critical point in making your decision is that whatever policy you adopt, assume it will be widely used and it should be applied consistently and fairly amongst the family. This is a case where fairness and consistency are as important as the result. And if you make loans to some family members, they should be documented as if they were made on an arm's-length business and fully disclosed to all family members. Disclosure helps prevent rumors, misunderstandings, and jealousies.

Any loan policy has to be thought through wisely because if some shareholders avail themselves of the opportunity to borrow from the business, many may want to do so—especially if the business is paying small dividends and if you have shareholders not working in the business. Do not set yourself up for the proverbial "run on the bank."

Most of my clients do not have a family loan policy. Most, after thinking through the issue, have decided that in those cases where family members need help, it is the duty of the parents or siblings to help; they believe that this is easier and less problematic than a family loan policy.

The business's purchase of services or products from other businesses owned by some family members is more common. Office supplies, insurance, legal advice, accounting services, travel, landscaping, architectural, floral, decorating, and real estate brokerage are all common services needed by most businesses.

This issue arises in almost every case where you have a multi-generational family business with a large number of family shareholders not working in the business. It also arises frequently where sons and grand-sons work in the business and daughters do not but their husbands oper-ate independent businesses providing services that the family business may need. Most people are puzzled by why this is even an issue. They think that if a business has to buy a product or service, it should buy it from fam-ily.

Trust me, if you have family shareholders not working in the business and if you pay minimal dividends, then any money—yes, any money—flowing out of the business to any shareholder for any reason will raise is-sues of "What do I get from the business?" and "What benefits do I receive?"

For those reasons you should adopt and disclose a policy regarding the purchase of goods and services from family members and that policy should be fairly and consistently applied. Such policy should state that all such transactions will be on an arm's-length basis at market prices for com-parable services and all such purchases should be disclosed to all share-holders.

Closely aligned to this issue is the issue of whether the family business should invest in entrepreneurial ventures or business start-ups owned by family members or in-laws? This is a more difficult issue, especially in the case where you have many family shareholders. Non-core business invest-ments are a discretionary use of family shareholders' money—an invest-ment decision. Some of my clients have decided that the business should not be an investment vehicle but that each family member should make their own investments using their own moneys based on their individual risk/return parameters and tolerances. In such cases, all family members could be given the opportunity to invest personally in a separate venture on the same basis. Or, I have had families create a separate investment fund for entrepreneurial investments with moneys contributed by interested and willing family members.

The key point to remember in making family business investment deci-sions is that while you may be the CEO or the FBL, the money belongs to all the shareholders—NOT just you. You can advise, recommend, and opine but you cannot appropriate their money.

The last common perk or benefit to be discussed is charitable contribu-tions. Most family businesses want to be seen as good corporate and com-munity citizens and accordingly, make or sponsor charitable contributions. This is not an issue. However, when the family business has many family shareholders, the designation of those charities can be both an opportunity for family disagreement and the opportunity to provide some emotional benefits to family shareholders not working in the business.

It is not unusual for successful families to have family members involved in their own chosen charities. People sometimes seek out meaningful charities that can be their individual opportunity to represent the family in the community and to have status. And if you have several family members active in several different charities, it is not unusual that each wants the business's contributions to be made to their specific charity because in most cases the amount of the contribution impacts leadership, publicity, and status opportunities. Again, the family business "money pie" is only so big. Whose favorite charities get chosen?

One of my clients created a charitable contribution shareholder committee that decides contributions on a rotating basis. Another of my clients decided that the business would make contributions that help the business, not individual shareholders. Another client decided that this was the way to give some benefits to shareholders not working in the business and makes contributions based on that basis.

Chapter 8

Sibling and Cousin Rivalries

The complex inter-dynamics of managing both the family and the business arises whenever siblings or cousins choose to join the family business. Family rivalries are caused by two fundamental facts:

- Human nature
- Ultimately, there is only one CEO position available for a family member.

Every person wants the opportunity to prove him or herself—the opportunity to earn the respect of their peers and parents. Children of successful family business builders want to earn their family's respect and want the opportunity to be judged on their own merits. Yes, people want to win and be better than other family members.

Unfortunately, in most businesses there can only be one CEO—one head person—one boss. It is this inherent limitation on top management positions that creates the competition for those positions amongst family members. Rivalries will happen; they are normal and are a given. The issue for family business leaders is how do you manage them and how do you organize or structure people's roles so as to minimize the potential negative or destructive aspects of rivalries.

I have spent so much time over the years dealing with rivalry issues that my experience has led me to use the term "sandbox theory" to explain a way to manage rivalries. What have I learned? *Every family member needs his or her own sandbox. And family members generally do not share sandboxes well.* What do I mean by "own sandbox"? Each family member working in the business ultimately needs their own discrete, separate area of responsibility in which no other family member operates. It is this concept learned

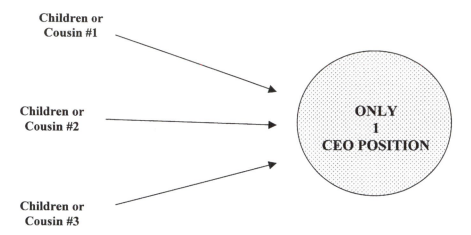

Figure 8.1. Competition for the Leadership Position

from experience that is the underlying principle of how I advise clients dealing with multiple siblings or cousins working in the business.

In addition, there are some common sense rules that I have found helpful in organizing or structuring how you employ siblings or cousins. First, siblings or cousins should not report to or be managed by other siblings or cousins, and secondly, siblings should not be managed by their parents, if at all possible.

Many families try to resolve rivalry issues through the sharing of power and responsibility through co-positions such as co-CEOs. Although there are cases in the public literature where siblings have been able to work well together and share power, my experience is that co-CEOs and co-presidents just have not worked. It is rare to find two high achievers who can subvert their egos to the good of the whole—the family—over an extended period of time.

How can you implement my sandbox theory? How does it apply to operating and managing a business? By giving each family employee ultimately their own sandbox. And a separate, distinct sandbox can be a separate business function or a separate product line or service responsibilities, or separate geographical or branch responsibilities.

By business functions, I mean sales, finance, manufacturing, human resources, legal, real estate. By geographical, I mean separate territories, separate locations or regions. Try to structure the business so that each sibling or cousin has their own distinct area of responsibility where they can be judged objectively on their performance.

Well known in the public press are some very wealthy families who historically have evolved to the sandbox theory to give each family sibling his or her own distinct business to manage. The clearest example of the sandbox theory is the split of the Bass Family fortune in the mid 1980s into separate entities, giving each of the four Bass Brothers their own autonomy and distinct entity.

On much smaller scales, here are several other examples of the sandbox theory. Company "A" was a second-generation family business with approximately 26 shareholders, 4 of which worked full-time in the business. The 4 family members were either brothers, cousins, or a brother-in-law. How did they split up running the business—both by function and by geography? Everyone had their distinct non-overlapping job responsibility for which they were solely responsible. And it worked. There was no overlap and as importantly, no ambiguity internally in the company or externally in the marketplace or the community about each individual's role. Each had the title of vice president and each was paid the same salary.

Company "B" was a multi-billion dollar private family company that was managed by a son and son-in-law. The son was an arrogant, bright, hard charger who was long on criticism and short on "thank you's" and praise for employees. His brother-in-law was completely different. The brother-in-law was a kind, humble, gentle man who was loved by his employees. He was smart and as effective as the arrogant brother but with a different management style. How did these two so very different people co-exist? By each having their own sandbox. The company's operations were divided into five separate functions and the son ran three functions and the son-in-law ran two functions and the functions were integrated and communicated to each other through their second tier management teams—not through the two senior executives. It worked beautifully. No matter the topic, it belonged primarily in one of the five functions and each respected each other's turf—space. In working with that company for over five years on strategic issues and capital issues, I never participated in any meeting where both the son and the son-in-law were present.

Company "C" was a third generation private family business owned by two sisters who inherited the business from their father. The family was facing a potential divisive battle over who would succeed the husband. One branch of the family had no qualified candidates. The other branch had two qualified candidates—siblings. The older brother thought by right he should be the heir apparent. The younger brother was not challenging his older brother to be the successor. But all of his cousins wanted the younger brother to be the new CEO and they were strongly opposed to the older brother. A classic opportunity for a major dispute.

This family was smart. They solved their problem with the sandbox theory. They split off from the main business an ancillary separate business and allowed the older brother to run it completely separate and distinct from the core business, which the younger brother was chosen to run as CEO.

Company "D" was a major beer distributor. That family split up family responsibilities along geographical lines. Each family member managed a separate autonomous geographical market.

Family business leaders need to understand that rivalries are common and need to be proactively and preemptively managed. The sandbox theory is responsive to every individual's need for autonomy, the need to prove oneself and earn the love and respect of one's family and peers.

Remember, employing multiple family members will increase the likelihood of rivalries. So manage that likelihood preemptively and proactively. Give everybody their own separate, distinct sandbox.

Chapter 9

Stock Ownership and Liquidity

The ownership of stock in a family business presents difficult questions for many families. Some of these questions are:

- Should spouses of family members own stock?
- May family business stock be sold to non-family members?
- Should non-family senior management own stock?
- What restrictions should be placed on stock transfers?
- How is the stock valued?
- What happens to the stock upon death, disability, or divorce?
- Should stock ownership be restricted to those family members working in the business?

The ownership of stock represents the right to a pro rata share of wealth being created. How does a family shareholder with a small ownership position realize or actualize that value? Unlike owning stock in a public company, most family businesses have no public market, trading, or liquidity in their stock so the value of the stock is difficult to determine since no public market exists and in most cases there are no comparable sales of similarly situated stock. And that value is difficult to realize on an individual basis, i.e., turn it into cash because there is no established market of buyers.

Stock liquidity becomes very important to shareholders who are not employed in the business and who receive only minimal cash dividends. Such shareholders often ask themselves, "Why should I own this stock? Why not sell the stock and at least get cash for a house down payment, a new car, graduate school, private schooling for children, or college education funds?"

As you can see, the ownership of stock and what it represents is a much more complex issue than most families expect. The ownership of stock in a family business is a legal relationship between the company, majority family shareholders, and minority family shareholders. Shareholders have legal rights under federal and state corporation and securities laws. Minority shareholders are owed fiduciary duties by the majority. Why is this important? Because you need to understand the various rights and obligations owed to minority shareholders as you decide who can own stock and under what restrictions.

Most families I have worked with had previously decided that their children and their spouses can own or control stock in their own right and as trustees of grandchildren's trusts. Few families have policies dealing with divorce; even fewer have prenuptials; and few have liquidity options. Most family businesses have some restrictions and limitations on the transfer or sale of family business stock and a few have stock valuation formulas to be used for gift tax purposes and for internal family transfer or sale purposes. Most do not have a stock buy-back plans.

My consulting experiences the last 10 years have changed my views dramatically on the issues of stock ownership and stock liquidity. Too many families cavalierly make gifts of family business stock to children, grandchildren, and trusts motivated solely by estate tax purposes and fail to comprehend the highly likely powerful, disruptive forces they are creating that could limit the legacy of the family business.

As the number of shareholders expands and as the number of family shareholders not working in the business expands, those shareholders will first put pressure on the family business to pay meaningful dividends and ultimately, if not satisfied, will put pressure on the family business for stock liquidity. These pressures, if not managed, can lead to pressures to sell the business or to buy out frustrated shareholders.

Two examples:

Company "A" was created as an investment vehicle by a father for his five children. Quite wonderfully, that company grew into quite a large business that was run by the older brother. The other four siblings did not work in the business. Three were full-time moms and a younger brother was a musician. The stock of this business represented by far the vast majority of wealth for each of the four siblings not working in the business.

The elder brother basically ran the business that supported five families. As the siblings aged, the need for house down payments, bigger houses, private school tuitions, etc. all put more and more pressure on the elder brother to generate and pay bigger dividends. Pressure included monthly and in some cases, weekly calls for money by his siblings. Not surprisingly, two brothers-in-law first raised the issue of stock liquidity. Because of these family demands, the family company was sold and each sibling received his or her share of the proceeds upon which to live.

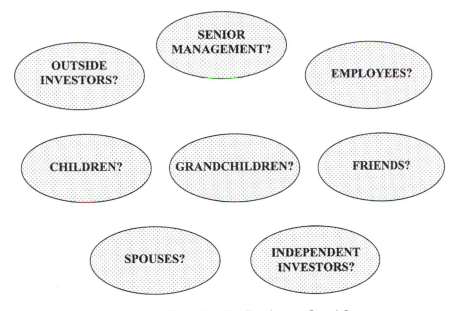

Figure 9.1. Who Should Own Family Business Stock?

Company "B" was a second generation family business with 25 family members as shareholders, 21 of which did not work in the business. After 5 years of pleading to no avail for larger dividends and some stock liquidity, the 21 forced the sale of the company.

Company "C" is a fifth generation family business with 175 family shareholders and a non-family CEO. Younger shareholders are living all across the United States. What does stock ownership represent to them? What are their cash needs? That family business, in order to keep family peace, has embarked on a 5-year plan to distribute increasingly meaningful cash dividends and is putting in place a stock buy-back plan.

Who should own the stock of a family business? Should in-laws, third parties, outsiders, non-family management be allowed to own stock? My advice on this issue is quite conservative. A family business is family—direct descendants. Stock ownership, for risk management purposes, should be limited to direct family members. In-laws, outsiders, independent directors, non-family management, and employees should not own stock in a family business.

Not all my clients follow this advice. Some allow senior non-family management to own stock. Some allow divorced ex in-laws to own stock. Some allow stock to be bequeathed to anyone. Why does this concern me? Having minority non-family member shareholders in a family business increases the risk of disputes and lawsuits. The family owes fiduciary duties to such non-family shareholders and as a result, every transaction, payment, or exchange between the business and any family member should be solely for business purposes, on an arm's-length basis at market rates and be fair. Depending on the size of the transaction, to protect minority shareholders, a fairness opinion by independent objective advisors may be required. Secondly, family shareholders receive family emotional benefits from stock ownership. Stock ownership for non-family members is purely an investment. Such non-family shareholders may not be as patient with the lack of dividends, or the small amount of dividends, or the lack of marketability of the stock at reasonable values. Non-family shareholders may contest family salaries, perks, and benefits. In addition, the stock could be part of a contested divorce or a trustee trying to force the sale of the stock.

If your goal is to build a legacy family business—one that will last beyond one generation—you should be aware that non-family shareholders will make that goal more difficult to achieve.

Should family stock ownership be limited to family members working in the business? This is a much more complex question because the answer depends in part on what is the purpose of the family business and in part on how a family deals with inheritance equity amongst family members. What percent of the family's wealth does the business represent? Does the family have enough non-family business assets to treat family members not working in the business fairly from an inheritance viewpoint?

By now you should be thinking that stock ownership is much more complex than you thought. Yes, it is. But do not despair—it can work beautifully. I have several multi-generational family businesses with many shareholders not working in the business that are working well. They are working well because the family has taught the shareholders the value of stewardship and because the family directly, frequently, and openly talks abut the dividend issue and the stock liquidity issue and they work hard at educating and communicating with family shareholders not involved in the business on a frequent basis. They have plans in place to deal with dividend pressures and stock liquidity needs.

Once you decide who may own stock in your family business, then you need to decide what restrictions should be placed on the transfer of that stock. Family business stock should not be transferred, sold, pledged, gifted, donated to any person, entity, or charity unless that person is a family member who can own the stock. Most such stock restrictions allow for gifts to children and to trusts for minors.

What about non-family employees and senior management. My advice again is conservative—they are not family and they should not own stock. You can compensate them fully for adding value using other compensation techniques besides direct stock ownership. Phantom stock plans can work well.

Many times I am asked about whether family members should have the right to sell their stock to anyone so long as they first offer to sell the stock to other family members on the same terms—i.e., a right of first refusal. My advice is no. Non-family shareholders are not family and may have different objectives than the family. Secondly, non-family shareholders will be owed minority shareholder fiduciary duties and have the right to question any financial dealings or transaction between any family member and the business. Families sometimes make business decisions taking into account family needs and such decisions may seem unwise or poor business judgments to non-family member shareholders.

What about divorce? Family business stock should not be transferred in a divorce to a non-family member ex-spouse. Other assets should be utilized to meet those marital obligations.

How about prenuptials dealing with family business stock? Although I have had many clients talk about and think about "requiring" their children to have signed prenuptial agreements in place before marrying, I know of only one case where it was actually done and the children were told of this family requirement—the process of communicating and educating why it is necessary—before the children went to college. In other words, it was an adopted family business policy before the son met Ms. Right. So that family tried to depersonalize the prenuptial by having a long-standing written family business policy that applied to all children and cousins that was put in place when the children were teenagers.

Widely held stock within a multi-generational family creates pressure not only for dividends but also for liquidity. This is especially the case where you have young adult shareholders wanting their first house or needing moneys for schooling young children. They can view the family business as less important or meaningful and have less of an emotional attachment to it, especially if they are not involved in the business on a daily basis and even more so if they live in a city remote from the business.

My clients who have had these facts have historically gone through predictable reactions to young shareholders' demands for some tangible financial benefit from the business. The first response usually is "this is a problem for their parents—they should handle it." The second response usually is "that is the reality of owning illiquid stock in a family business—they should be thankful they were given the stock." Then a senior family member usually asks a good question, "Do we want to force family members to stay on as shareholders if they really do not want to be involved in the business?" It is hard enough to manage a business and the family who want to be involved. It is even harder to "manage" unhappy family shareholders.

Most families I have worked with end up agreeing that unhappy, uninvolved family shareholders should have the opportunity to sell their stock to either the family business or to another family member. Then they go through a process that begins with the unhappy shareholders offering to sell his or her stock to his or her parents and if they do not want to buy the stock, then it is then offered to siblings in order to keep the ownership ratio between branches of the family the same. In many cases, parents do not want to buy the stock because of estate tax issues and siblings do not have the cash. Then everyone starts looking for a source of cash and thus, the business becomes the likely buyer. But the management of the business becomes concerned—what if many shareholders want to sell at the same time and we have a "run on the business treasury."

They are right. Any stock liquidity plan or stock buy-back plan has to take into account the relative ownership amongst family members or branches and also the amount of available, free cash flow in the business that can be allocated for this use—keeping in mind the business's working capital needs and growth needs as well as the amount of cash needed to pay dividends.

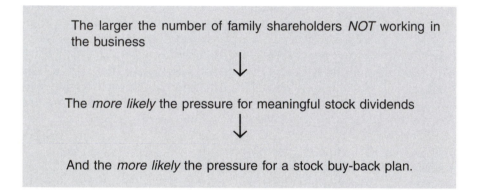

The larger the number of family shareholders *NOT* working in the business

↓

The *more likely* the pressure for meaningful stock dividends

↓

And the *more likely* the pressure for a stock buy-back plan.

Many stock buy-back plans contain provisions setting forth the maximum number of shares the company is obligated to buy each year and how that amount would be allocated amongst shareholders wanting to sell in a given year. Should you buy the stock back with company debt? My advice is no. Unhappy creditors can create more business problems than unhappy shareholders. Creditors can sue if a principle or interest payment is in default.

In most family businesses, there is a limit—a finite amount of cash available in any given year—to fund stock buy-backs. And if you get this far, having decided that it really makes no sense long-term to force or require unhappy family shareholders to remain as shareholders and that it makes sense to provide some type of pro rata, affordable liquidity that is funded either by other family members or by the business, you will then get to the issue of how do you value an illiquid minority interest in a family business?

The valuation of stock in a public company is easy—one uses price/earnings ratios or a discounted cash flow basis or a multiple of EBITDA (earnings before interest, taxes, depreciation, and amortization). Or one looks at recent sales of the stock for comparables.

Well, there is no public market for a private family business and in most cases no comparable transactions. Thus, families with the help of tax, legal, and financial advisors have to agree upon a formula for valuation to be used in all cases that takes into account the business, its industry, its prospects, its risks, its illiquidity, and the fact that a minority non-controlling block of stock will be sold. This valuation formula is important because it should be used in all cases of stock transfers for all purposes. In other words, one should not use one formula for gift tax purposes and a different formula for a sale back to the company.

My experience is that it takes time for families to work through the valuation issue because individual family members' positions or opinions change as they change their viewpoint from that of a potential buyer to a potential seller. Ultimately, the goal should be fairness and reasonableness for both buyer and seller. Selling shareholders want a high value, and buying shareholders want a low value. Many stock valuation formulas in their adoption are motivated by gift tax purposes to produce low valuations. When people decide to sell, they are usually unhappy with that valuation.

The real question is what is the fair discount to be placed on the value of the stock because of its illiquidity and minority position. And this discount has to be fair because today's buyer could be tomorrow's seller.

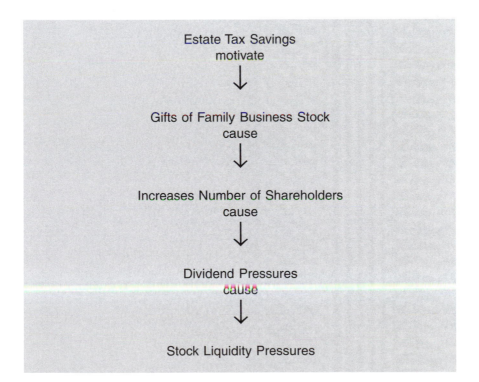

What happens if you have many shareholders who want to sell—more sellers than buyers and more sellers than cash available in the business. You need to think through those issues before you adopt a stock repurchase plan. At what point do you just sell the business? At what point do you borrow money to buy out unhappy shareholders? Or at what point do you require them to sell over time so the business can afford it over time?

It should be obvious to you by now that unhappy shareholders can create major problems. One of the main purposes of this book is to promote the concept that the proactive and preemptive active management of these family business issues will increase the probability of your family business remaining successful and harmonious.

Successful legacy family businesses understand that individual family members' needs will change as they age and that shareholders not involved in the family business on a daily basis will have different needs and views from those shareholders working in the business. And these different perspectives must be respected, talked about, and dealt with.

Chapter 10

Board of Directors

A Board of Directors is the shareholders' elected representatives who oversee the management of the business. In young family businesses, the board is made up usually of family members—sometimes all shareholders if a small number. As the family business grows, some families ask non-family member advisors, such as lawyers and accountants, to serve on the board.

Lastly, as the family matures and if the family business has been fortunate enough to survive generational changes and leadership succession, the issue of board membership and structure become more complex. The questions become whether board composition should mirror or represent the age, gender, and family branch demographics of the shareholders. And if during the previous leadership transition, outside (non-family) senior management has been hired, should the board have qualified independent directors to oversee such management?

Obviously, the answers to these questions depends upon many factors:

- The number of shareholders;
- The number of generations and branches of the family represented;
- The qualifications of the shareholders;
- The number of family shareholders not working in the business; and
- The willingness of people to serve.

Historically, in many family businesses, Boards of Directors have been perfunctory ratification boards since the board members usually were the family members running the business—so they approved and ratified what they already had done.

But as the business world has become more volatile and hyper-competitive and as families have aged and grown, the composition of the board and its duties have become issues in every family business I have worked with over the past ten years. All of my multi-generation family businesses with over 20 shareholders have either restructured their board or they are in the process of doing so to make the board more demographically representative of the shareholders. For many family businesses, which are sometimes patriarchal, hierarchical, and seniority power based, this is a major change—almost revolutionary.

Some examples: Company A is a very successful, private family business, having lasted for three generations. The business has approximately 160 family shareholders. Historically, board members were elected based on seniority, branch representation, and business acumen. Over the years, this produced a "good ole boys" club of directors, all males over the age of 55.

As the family has grown and with the various branches making gifts of family business stock to younger generations, the number of family shareholders under the age of 50 far exceeds the number over the age of 50 and not surprisingly, the percentage of female shareholders is about 30 percent—with there never having been a female board member. And the number of shareholders not working in the business numbers 157. This family was having the common problem of younger family shareholders being unhappy with minimal dividends and the lack of stock liquidity. Their emotional connectedness to the business was tenuous.

These issues were real but they were the surface issues. The underlying issues were that younger shareholders and female shareholders wanted to be heard—wanted to have their views represented—they wanted to have their seat at the board table. In effect, there was a growing undercurrent of shareholder revolt against the "good ole boys" club.

The board's first reaction to hearing these views directly from courageous young and/or female shareholders was that they should wait their turn. Some board members viewed the complaints as petty. But the chairman of the board saw the potential for major future issues and the risk to his legacy as board chairman—that the family and the business could continue to prosper together after his tenure.

Once the board focused on its duties of stewardship and the need to involve all the shareholders in the family business, the board set about to restructure its membership so as to be more inclusive—inclusive of female shareholders, inclusive of younger shareholders, and inclusive of family members who were not experienced, successful business people.

Another of my clients—Company B—has about 30 shareholders, representing two branches of a family. Each branch has gifted stock to the third and fourth generations, including daughters and granddaughters. Many of the daughters are married and each branch has one younger shareholder working in the business.

The chairman of the board was a very enlightened man. He wanted more than anything for the family business to stay successful and to be a family legacy—to pass on to future generations. And he knew that the odds were against that unless the family was involved, and unless the family viewed the business as important and as more than just a piggy bank.

He very deliberately structured his Board so that each branch of the family had equal representation and within each branch there was female and younger generation representation. Each branch of the family has two female shareholders on the board and each branch has at least two generations on the board.

Many of my more traditional clients immediate reactions to these types of boards are: board meetings will take longer because we will have to explain more to the younger members or the inexperienced members. My response is yes and that is good because educated and informed shareholders are better for the long-term health of the business and the family than ignorant shareholders.

Some respond that younger or inexperienced board members will not keep family matters as confidential as older members. My experience is to the contrary. Others respond that by choosing a few younger shareholders, others' feelings will be hurt. My response is that *all* of them are currently excluded and that is more hurtful.

I have attended over the years several board meetings of Company B and am proud to report that the family got it right. The diverse family board worked in their case and it was interesting to see how hard the inexperienced members worked and studied in order to improve their business knowledge and skills.

Watching that board interact, it is clear that the chairman had institutionalized at the board level the duties of stewardship and the values of listening with respect and being open to different views and perspectives. The interchanges are honest, differing, but respectful and never ad personae. Questions, dissent, constructive critiques are welcomed. That family is lucky to have a 70-year-old chairman who has remained open to change and input, and who keeps his eye on the main goal of having a successful business and a harmonious family shareholder group.

After family representation by generation, branch, age, and gender, the next most common issue in Board structure is whether family businesses should have independent directors on their Boards.

Independent directors are generally non-family members who have knowledge and experience that may be valuable in overseeing the management of the company. In theory, I have historically liked the concept of independent directors for growing family businesses because many of the issues faced during growth phases, business plateau phases, and regeneration phases are the same for most businesses. Having the input of others who have successfully faced such issues makes sense to me. In many cases, running a business as the CEO can be a lonely job because many CEOs have no one at the company that they can be open and honest with concerning

Table 10.1
Board Matrix

By Gender	Working in Business	Not Working in Business
1st Generation		
2nd Generation		
3rd Generation, etc.		

their fears, problems, and competitive threats. CEOs generally need someone as a sounding board, someone to test and debate ideas with.

Most of my larger family business clients have independent board directors. A few of my clients believe they have the talent and independent views within the family shareholder group and thus, do not need independent directors.

My experience, however, with independent board members has been disappointing because in most of these cases they do not fulfill their function. I think there are three fundamental reasons for this. First, most family businesses choose their lawyer or their accountant to serve on the board. My experience is that in most cases, these advisors are as worried about offending the CEO as they are worried about doing their job. They are consciously or subconsciously worried about offending the CEO, or the family, and losing their fees. Many deal with this conflict by expressing their views "off-line"—after the board meeting to a receptive Director.

Secondly, in some cases, the CEO and chairman have never created the atmosphere or culture of critical inquiry and debate and the board remains a prefunctionary rubber stamp for the CEO. This is a waste of everyone's time. The ground rules, roles, and expectations of board participation need to be communicated and acted on. Good critical questions should be welcomed and expected.

Thirdly, being a good board member takes time and is hard work. And independent directors should be paid accordingly—in cash—after each board meeting. Too many of my clients in effect get what they pay for; i.e., they pay minimal director fees (such as $2500 per year) and they get what they pay for—minimal work.

Who is the right independent director? What should they be paid? A good independent director would be a person of impeccable integrity, judgment, and experience who has built and run successful businesses and who is independently wealthy and retired and is looking to be a mentor and coach. In such a case, you are buying wisdom, judgment, and "been-there-done-that" experience. What should he or she be paid? It depends on the size and complexity of your business, but a good range is $10,000–$25,000 per year, depending on the time commitment.

Let me share with you an article I wrote on independent directors for *The Catalyst Magazine* in March 2003.

INDEPENDENT DIRECTORS: PRIVATE COMPANIES NEED THEM, TOO

Private growth companies need independent directors either formally as part of the Board or informally as an Advisory Board as much or even more than public companies. The private company reasons, however, differ in most cases from public company needs. Entrepreneurs need independent objective advice from seasoned wise business builders. Entrepreneurs need reality checks; entrepreneurs need a check and balance mechanism; entrepreneurs need critical intellectual debate; entrepreneurs need someone to tell them what they need to hear, not necessarily what they want to hear; and entrepreneurs need advice on what does not work as much as what does work. That is the role of private company independent directors.

It's Lonely at the Top

Many leaders or business builders will tell you it is lonely at the top. How do you lead people and be their friend? How can you expect your employees and managers to be totally open, honest and direct with you when you control their paycheck? To whom do you turn to for straight talk, for a reality check, for dissent? With whom do you debate personnel issues? With whom do you debate ideas? With whom can you let your guard down in confidence and be totally open and honest?

That is why independent directors are so important. Business builders have strong personalities and they need reality checks frequently. They need sounding boards; they need to test their assumptions; they need a fresh pair of eyes and ears. Business builders need someone with whom they can let their guard down in confidence, be totally open and honest, and say, "I need some help here." Independent directors can meet those needs.

"Been There, Done That" Is Valuable Experience

In working with successful entrepreneurs, it is interesting how many have told me "I wish I had had a few successful business builders as mentors—people I could run ideas past—people who have dealt with the common issues: for example, when should I hire a real CFO; when do I put in formal HR policies and reviews; what has worked and not worked regarding team building; how do you keep employees motivated?"

Most businesses as they grow face similar issues at different stages of the life cycle regardless of their product or service. Whether they be marketing, finance, HR, internal controls, or employee morale, certain issues appear at different stages of everyone's growth cycle and those issues are generally related to the need for more organizational structure, more policies, and more controls as you grow. The balance between controls, systemic processes, and informality and flexibility is a constant tension.

Most entrepreneurs and business builders regardless of the stage of their company ($1 million in sales; $5 million; $25 million; or $100 million) are facing commonly occurring issues for the first time. Building a business is hard but it is not research microbiology or aeronautical engineering. You can save a lot of time, money, and trouble by learning from those who have been through what you are going through.

Business builders do not need the latest consulting fad or to be laboratories for the next strategy idea of the month. Business builders need wisdom and judgment from successful people who can listen, who have no underlying agenda, and who have "been there and done that." And for that wisdom and judgment to be valuable, the advice giver needs to be educated about your business, your people, and your industry so that he or she can respond quickly. That is why having these people serve on your board is wise—because it institutionalizes an education process so they are up to speed on you, your company, your results, and your issues. It prepares them to give you reasoned advice quickly. Find people who you can learn from.

Who and How Often?

Who? Clearly the ideal candidates are people who are knowledgeable about your industry, have a proven track record of business success, impeccable integrity, and the willingness to be an advisor, mentor, and straight shooter. It helps to have people who have experience in larger companies because they have dealt with some of the issues you will face as you grow. Find people with skills that you lack.

Look for diversity of experiences, in both business and life. Look for people who have overcome personal and business adversity that builds character. Look for people who have mentored others successfully. Look for "horses who have won different kinds of races."

How often? Growth companies need frequent board meetings to review progress and as a check and balance against the daily chaos. Entrepreneurs get very emotionally involved in building their business and their emotional involvement can impact decision making negatively if bias, rigidity of thinking, or arrogance sets in. Most people do not know what they do not know. Most people cannot step out of their own shoes and test reality and their underlying assumptions.

That is the purpose of monthly one-half day board meetings with independent, objective directors. Monthly meetings can institutionalize a rigorously applied reporting, critiquing, and intellectual debate process that entrepreneurs need.

Board meetings should be held quarterly and the board should take its oversight duties seriously. Besides financial results, business risks and threats, litigation, and growth issues the board should review and approve, if appropriate, any transaction involving the company and a family member and should continuously review dividend, stock liquidity, family employment, and succession issues.

Chapter 11

Succession

Most family businesses end at the founder's death and few make it through two leadership successions. I have been very fortunate to work with many third and fourth generation family businesses—those who have survived the passing of business founders and family leaders. About one half of these businesses have remained family-led and as you may surmise, the other half has hired outside non-family management.

Succession is a dual leadership change. A change in the leadership of the business and in some cases, a change in the leadership of the family. A leadership change at the business level can impact the business's strategy and culture as the new leader attempts to make his or her mark. Succession can be a change for the family as well since different people have different leadership styles and abilities to deal with family members and their business related issues. Often overlooked, succession can be a major individual change for the retiring CEO and for the incoming CEO. The retiring CEO is moving on to a different phase of his or her life and the incoming CEO is undertaking the heavy burden of being responsible for the family's wealth in the form of the business. The potential for upheaval in the business or in the family is high. Potential high-risk scenarios include:

- An elderly CEO refuses to retire and a frustrated qualified family successor leaves the business;
- The family CEO becomes incapacitated or dies unexpectedly and there is no obvious family successor;
- The family CEO becomes disabled and a family battle results over choosing one of the children or cousins as successor;
- The family CEO retires in name only and interferes and undermines the new CEO;

- The family is deadlocked and cannot choose a successor;
- The family hastily hires an unproven outside CEO who quickly wants to make major changes; or
- The family refuses to honestly and realistically evaluate family members and chooses a non-qualified family CEO successor who quickly makes bad business decisions.

Any discussion of succession must first start with the issue of retirement and a family policy for retirement. The next issue involves what I call the "duality" principle in that any succession involves two transitions—the transitioning out of the current leader to something meaningful in his or her life and the transitioning in of the new leader in such a manner to increase the probability of a successful succession. Most successful transitions take time and involve processes designed to increase the probability of success. And lastly, retirement policies and succession planning are integrally related to estate and financial planning and to the question of who will control the stock of the business.

Succession can be of two kinds—successions of position, such as naming a new CEO, and succession of stock control, which occur when the new CEO acquires a substantial or meaningful block of family business stock.

The issue of retirement can be a difficult issue. When is it time for a family leader to move on and pass on the family legacy? The right time depends upon the condition of the business, its near-term prospects, the health, productivity and effectiveness of the current leader, and whether a qualified, tested, and trusted successor is in place to keep the family business prosperous.

We have all heard of family business leaders who stayed on beyond their time—beyond their effectiveness and who could not let go—who could not pass on the position or power since the business was their life. Being needed, feeling useful and important, and the fear of mortality are all normal human emotions.

My experience is that the succession issue is primarily an emotional maturity issue and a values issue. "Me" oriented, self-centered leaders tend to want to hang on to the position and power as long as possible while "we" oriented, stewardship- and legacy-oriented family leaders proactively plan for the successful passing on of the position and power.

Succession planning is one of the most important duties of a family business leader and the planning should begin early in the business's life cycle. The family leader and the board of directors should have a succession plan in place when the family business leader is in his or her 40s in the unlikely event of an unexpected death and that plan should designate a CEO or an interim CEO until either a long-term CEO is found or until the business is sold.

And as the family business leader ages, the discussion of an Annual Succession Plan with the board should focus on either internal family or employee candidates or maybe an external candidate. And as the family business leader reaches age 50–55, by then the family starts seriously considering and preparing a family successor or starts a process to bring a non-family member into the company for a testing period.

Successful successions take at least 5 years—that is, either a potential family member or a non-family member successor needs a testing and training period before the succession occurs and the retiring CEO needs time to have transitioned his life so he or she has something meaningful to move on to.

Yes, a succession involves two moves by two people—a successor moving in and the retiree moving on and the moving on process is as important to the success of a succession as picking the right successor. In order for a succession to happen in reality, the retiree needs something meaningful to move on to—a new challenge in either, for example, charity work, education, politics, public service, conservation, or farming.

Most of my multi-generational family businesses have adopted mandatory ages of retirement of 70 years for the CEO-chairman and all have in recent years abided by the policy. The time to think about such a policy is long before the founder reaches 70 because it may be more difficult to put a policy in place that is used to retire one person quickly or saying it another way, it is far easier to adopt retirement policies that may apply to you in more than ten years.

Retirement policies have to be motivated and discussed in terms of stewardship and legacy and not personalized. Personalization could lead to hurt feelings and families being split over these difficult issues. There is a famous public family dispute that occurred in the Washington, DC area that involved the Haft family where a family sued each other over these types of issues with the mother and older son suing the father and younger son.

Having a retirement policy with a set age focuses the family leader and the Board on succession. Succession planning is not a 1-year or 2-year process because you need to build into your planning process a time period for testing the potential successor and room for error—your first choice of a successor may not work out and you want the testing period to occur while the current CEO is still in place.

Successors, whether from within the family or a non-family successor, should have worked in the company or intimately with the company for a substantial period of time—say 5 years as a general rule. By doing so, he or she will know the business and will have earned the respect and trust of employees, the shareholders, and the customers. You want enough time to test out two candidates, if necessary.

It is too risky to put an unproven person, regardless of family relationship, in the CEO position. Remember that succession will impact the family's financial net worth and legacy dramatically, either positively or negatively.

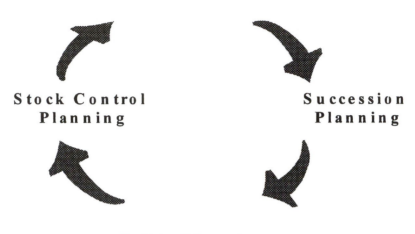

Figure 11.1. The Circle of Succession Planning

An integral part of succession planning for the family and for estate planning purposes is the issue of what happens to the founder's family business stock upon his or her retirement and related to that issue is what stock ownership position should the new family CEO own?

As you can imagine, there is no one answer to the stock ownership issue. It depends in part on the number of family shareholders, number of children and grandchildren, inheritance equity amongst children, whether the retiring CEO and his or her spouse have adequate financial resources independent of the business for retirement, and whether the business or any other shareholder can afford to purchase the stock or whether the family has had in place a long-term gifting program.

Another way to analyze the stock ownership issue is to ask the question, what does the stock represent to the retiring CEO? Is the stock a necessary income generator through dividends? Is the stock a means of control—controlling either the family or the business? Or is it one of many assets that the retiring CEO and spouse can utilize to pass on wealth to their heirs?

If the stock represents income through dividends that the retiring CEO and spouse need to meet living expenses, then the retiring CEO and spouse need to retain the stock until they both die—unless the business or their children can buy the stock for enough cash to replace the amount of dividends for both the CEO and spouse's lives.

The ownership of stock not only has financial implications but it also has control of the business implications. Should the retiring chairman/CEO be able to control the election of the board and corresponding election of officers through stock control? Should the retiring chairman/CEO stay on as chairman of the board?

The answer to these questions depends in large part on whether the retiring CEO will in fact retire to a non-executive chairman's post and perform only the duties of the chairman of the board and not use that position to continue to operate the business on a daily basis. In many cases, it is hard for a retiring CEO to let go. In many cases, even the retiring CEO does not know whether he or she can let go. For many business builders, the business is their life—their reason for living and they do not know how or with what to replace the business in their life.

So succession planning involves *both*:

- The issues of transferring daily leadership and management of the business; and
- The issues of how and when to transfer stock ownership of the business to succeeding generations.

Let me stress that the transfer of stock involves two separate issues: when and how.

Most families have at least three choices regarding how or in what manner to transfer the stock ownership plan.

The first choice is to transfer the stock pro rata to all children, i.e., equal ownership; the second choice is to transfer stock ownership to all children with the successor CEO child receiving a larger ownership position; and third, transfer all the stock to children working in the business and transfer a like amount of other assets to children not working in the business.

The question of "when" is dependent on the retiring CEOs financial situation and family circumstances. "When" is a very personal issue. For many reasons—financial, emotional, the inability of children or the business to buy the stock for its value at this time, and for tax planning reasons, most of my clients have chosen to retain their stock interest upon retirement and to let the stock pass on pursuant to their estate plan.

This is important because it is rare that a family business has the excess cash to fund dividends, retirements, stock repurchases, and business needs. Planning is key and here you need sophisticated, experienced legal and tax advisors who can help you put in place an integrated coordinated financial, estate, tax, and legal plan to preserve and protect what you have built for your loved ones.

Succession planning is like insurance—it protects the family from financial value destruction.
Succession planning should be depersonalized. It is the essence of stewardship.
The board of directors should approve a succession plan annually.

Throughout this book, I have stressed that the role of the family business leader is to manage *both* the family and the business. We have discussed that the management of the family is different from managing the business and takes specific skills and competencies. In choosing a successor family leader, you should keep in mind both of those functions and especially focus on the skills needed to manage the changing family dynamics.

Sometimes families have several younger family members working in the business and either an open or a covert competition amongst siblings or cousins taking place to be the successor family business leader. How can you, as family business leader, and the Board manage that competition so that the "losers" do not create family strife or business problems inside the company?

Again, it is by having an open, transparent process that sets forth upfront the qualifications, experience, skills, and competencies that the next family business leader should possess. In doing a competency need assessment, the Board should think about not only where is the business in its life cycle but also think about the family issues likely to arise over the next 5–10 years and the abilities needed to manage those family issues so as to preserve the family's values and its harmony. If the board educates and communicates these issues and the skills needed by the next CEO to all family shareholders and if all interested family candidates are given a fair opportunity in the interview and review process, most families either alone or with the help of an outside advisor can come to the "right" decision—picking the right person for that time.

What should the "losers" do? Quit the business and go elsewhere? I have seen that happen. But it is just as likely if the family has strong values and if each family member has his or her own "sandbox" in the business, that there is no reason why the loser(s) cannot continue to play an important role in the business and family. Sometimes not being chosen is a timing issue. Sometimes it is a skills or competencies issue. Situations change. People can learn new skills and competencies.

It all comes down to how the process is conducted—how the family shareholders are listened to—and how the individual candidates are treated. The groundwork should have been laid long ago by the family that there can only be one CEO and that how one conducts him or herself if chosen and if not chosen is important.

All along so far we have assumed that the family leader is wise and realistic about the need for succession planning. What if the family leader will not discuss succession? In this type of situation where the family business leader does not want to deal directly with his or her mortality and duty of stewardship, the spouse (usually wife) has to take the lead for the good of the family and try to persuade the CEO that he owes it to her and to the children to deal with this issue. Doing so lessens the financial risks to her and the family of an unexpected tragedy occurring with no likely successor in place. The lack of succession planning can result in a forced, hurried sale of the business and usually in those cases, value can be destroyed. If the CEO rebuffs those requests, then the family has no alternative but to create, with the help of advisors, their own succession plan.

CO-CEOs

Some families seek to avoid choosing between competing siblings or cousins and think about co-CEOs. There are instances of co-leaders working in the business world, but my experience has been that it takes two very special people to make it work and that in most cases, it does not work.

Should the retiring chairman/CEO family leader remain as chairman of the board? Again, depending on the individual facts and circumstances, remaining as chairman can either be a supportive event or a destructive event depending on the personalities and skills of both the retiring CEO and the incoming CEO. So long as the retiring CEO lets go and does not use the chairman's position to second-guess or micromanage the new CEO but rather is a supportive resource, it can work well for all involved.

I would like to share with you the story of a successful family succession involving one of my clients. This story is rich in family history being a third generation family business and is rich in emotional depth.

This is a story of a family succession where the retiring CEO kept his stock ownership and stayed on as chairman. The story will contain parts of an interview with the retiring CEO, the younger nephew of the retiring CEO who was chosen as successor CEO, and a senior family member not involved in the business on a daily basis. From this story, one can learn the importance of process—how it was done; of the duality principle—the retiring CEO having something meaningful to move on to; and the family's commitment to be a family company and a harmonious family. You will see the importance of planning the training of a successor, of that successor accepting the awesome responsibility and the power humbly and how he evolved into the role, how he took his time making changes, how he limited his changes in the beginning to those easily digestible by the business and the family and how his ego did not drive him to make the company "his." Rather, he understood that the "torch had been passed on to him" and his job was a stewardship job to play a key role growing the business and passing the torch to the next generation. Power did not go to the new CEOs head. He was and is a remarkable young man—comfortable with himself, confident, emotionally mature and as you will see, he understands the family business leader role and spends time educating and listening to family shareholders.

As the story of The Beach Company of Charleston, South Carolina, illustrates, successful family successions take planning, work, and time. Time to train and test the potential successor. Time for the retiree to create something to move on to. Planning how and when power will be transferred—how it will be passed and what the retiree can do to make it more likely to be successful. And what the successor needs to do to make it successful. Succession is stewardship and legacy building in action.

Chapter 12

Case Study: The Beach Company

Successful successions require family leaders to elevate at the appropriate time one's duty of stewardship to one's family and employees above one's personnel needs. Effective succession requires family leaders to realistically assess family members' abilities and readiness to ascend to the leadership role and to manage the process of either choosing one family member over another family member or informing family members that they will not be chosen as successor.

Then, one has to realistically assess the business needs going forward and recruit the right person with the right values and skills to lead the business and who will respect the family, the culture you have built, and who will understand the unique aspects of managing and leading a family business as an outsider. Lastly, then the family leader has to actually let go—give up the position, both internally and externally, and manage the success of the transition.

The Beach Company story is the story of two internal family successions and how two branches of a family have managed not only a family succession twice—a rare occurrence—but how they have wisely structured the families relationships and interaction with the Company to increase the probability that the family business will be a fourth generation business.

It is the story of two sisters and their husbands who have over the years negotiated and reached consensus compromise agreements on the issues of dividends, Board representation, family succession, charitable contributions, the families' roles in the community, limiting the number of family members to be employed in the Company, while implementing the "Sandbox Theory" two times.

And most of this has been done since 1997. First, some history and background. The Beach Company was founded in 1945 by former South Carolina State Senator John Charles (J.C.) Long when he purchased for approximately $100,000 the 2900-acre barrier isle north of Charleston named the Isle of Palms. J.C. had the foresight, entrepreneurial drive, legal knowledge, and political skills to purchase the piece of land and begun its development into an ultimate 5000 person community where beachfront lots today sell for over $3 million.

From that beginning in 1945, The Beach Company has grown to become the largest and most prestigious full service real estate firm in the Low Country of South Carolina with major commercial, residential, multifamily, retail, industrial and land development projects with over 300 employees in its leasing, brokerage, management, development, marina, and construction company divisions.

The Beach Company today manages over 3 million square feet of properties and has under construction over $150 million of new projects. It is financially very successful paying significant dividends to its shareholders while maintaining a strong and liquid balance sheet for future growth.

The Beach Company specializes in high profile unique class A developments in the Charleston area. Examples are:

- Seaside Farms, a 500-acre mixed use development;
- Majestic Square, an office and retail project anchored by the department store Saks Fifth Avenue, accompanied with a 472-car parking garage;
- Victoria Square, an office and retail complex anchored by Brooks Brothers;
- The Bristol, a condominium project along the Ashley River;
- Canon Place, a medical professional high rise near the Medical College of The University of South Carolina;
- Wild Dunes, the prestigious resort and residential community; and
- Kiawah, which the Company purchased in 1998 with Morgan Stanley Realty Partners for over $100 million, at the time the largest real estate transaction in the state of South Carolina. Today, Kiawah averages close to $300 million of residential sales annually and contains five world-class golf courses and was home to the Ryder Cup Competition.

The Beach Company's impact upon the Charleston community is not limited to real estate development. The Beach Company and its stock holders have given significant cash and in-kind property (millions) to Charleston charities and Charles S. Way, Jr., the Chairman of the Beach Company, is the past long-term President and Chairman Emeritus and builder of Charleston's internationally known culture festival—The Spoleto Festival USA.

Another key family leader and shareholder is Dr. Charles P. Darby, the retired head of MUSC Children's Hospital at the Medical College of South Carolina. The college recently honored Darby with the naming of its new pediatric research facility—The Charles P. Darby Children's Research Institute.

The Beach Company is owned by two branches or families—the Way Family and the Darby Family. J. C. Long, the founder, had two daughters: Mary Ellen and Joyce. Mary Ellen married a lawyer, Charles S. Way, Jr., and Joyce married a doctor, Charles P. Darby.

The Beach Company is owned today 50 percent by Way family members and 50 percent by Darby family members, totaling 14 shareholders. The number of family shareholders could, over the next 10 years, grow to more than 35 shareholders as the fourth generation reaches adulthood.

The Beach Company is managed by a Board of Directors configured of nine members—three Way family members, three Darby family members and three independent directors.

The Beach Company employs over 300 people, but it employs by shareholder agreement only family members who are qualified, experienced, and approved for employment by the Board of Directors. However, the Company does contract with a planning and landscape architectural firm owned by two sons-in-law (one Darby and one Way) and has a marina joint venture with a Way son-in-law.

The Beach Company has successfully navigated two family successors: from J. C. Long to his son-in-law, Charlie Way, in 1975 and 1984; and from Charlie Way to his nephew, John Charles Long Darby, in 1999 and 2002.

The Way and Darby families are involved in Charleston and South Carolina politics, government service, business, and philanthropic work, including Charlie Way's induction into the South Carolina Business Hall of Fame, being the recipient of not one but three of the Order of Palmetto, the highest honor given to any South Carolina resident, and he served as Secretary of Commerce of the State from 1999–2002. John Darby serves on many boards and recently chaired the Regional Economic Development Strategic Plan for the Charleston Region, the first time the competing regional government worked together for the good of the region.

I have mentioned Dr. Darby's honors previously. All of this is important because as we study how this family has successfully managed family issues from nepotism, to succession, to Board representation, to whose charities to sponsor, we will learn how this family so far has been able to place family harmony, stewardship, and family reputation, image and legacy above personal self-interest, ambition, and greed.

The Beach Company is the story of two families—two sisters who are very different. They have not only instilled values into their children while being in the "background," but also are today consulted on the strategic direction of the business. It is the story of two remarkable husbands—Charlie

Way and Dr. Darby—who never competed against each other, who understood each other's strengths, and who, at several critical times in the 60-year history, sat down and came to agreement of what was in the best interests of the whole family and the business and put aside loyalty to a particular son or daughter.

In 1997, the Beach Company was about one-half its current size. There were 14 family shareholders and the Board of Directors was not diverse from a gender or age perspective. Three family members worked in the business. Charlie Way (age 56) was president and CEO. Buddy Darby (age 42), John's older brother, was head of the Kiawah Resort Division and John Darby (age 33) worked in the development side of the business.

The Company had neither a business nor a family strategic succession plan. At that point, the Company paid family shareholders modest dividends. The family was struggling with the third generation connectedness to the business and the fact that the third generation had growing financial needs for houses and schooling.

In 1997, I began working with the Beach Company on their strategic business plan and on the issues of keeping the family involved and committed to the business. And over a six-year period, we dealt with many family business issues faced by all family businesses from succession, the Sandbox Theory, family employment, in-law issues, doing business with family-owned companies, allocation of charitable contributions, board representation, stock restrictions, family employee compensation, and family business communication processes.

During my first four months, I met individually with every family member (14) and individually with their spouses (14) to listen to their issues, concerns, and views on what the family business represented to them, what they wanted for the family business, what they wanted emotionally and financially from the family business, and how they wanted to be involved.

Out of this came a five-year strategic plan for the business that included stock dividend, stock restrictions, family succession, and family involvement plans. That plan was updated and revised in 2003.

The families used a business strategic planning process to ease into family issues. And the trust built by involving every family member and spouse set the precedent for how family issues should be dealt with and elevated the business over and above the personal financial self-interest of any individual shareholder.

As John Darby states today, "It was through this strategic planning process that a culture of family business discussion and debate was created and in which family members not involved in the business and spouses are given equal opportunity and equal respect to have input. This is critical to our ongoing business success and family harmony."

Because of the richness of this story and how much can be learned from this wonderful family, I want to share with you key comments made by five family members in March of 2005 as we reflected on how and why they have been able over the last seven and a half years to take the steps we have discussed. Part of the beauty and improbability of this story is the fact that every one of the 14 shareholders is a strong personality—their own individuals with passionately held views.

The younger women have strong leadership role models in Mary Ellen and Joyce. The younger men have role models who have been very successful in their own right in Charlie Way and Dr. Darby. All of the ten children want to be respected in the community and want to accomplish things in their areas of interest. For example, Anne Darby Parker created and led for 11 years the building of the Children's Museum of the Low Country.

Before proceeding, I want to emphasize that in 1997 this family had the potential and opportunity to act differently than they ultimately did. They, as a group, possessed all the usual human tendencies of ambition, self-interest, rivalries, jealousies, greed, the need for family recognition and respect, and the need to be seen in the community as a family leader. Added to this was disparity in wealth between generations and the disparity in the company benefits received by family members working in the business as compared to those not working in the business.

Wisdom, family leadership, and values trumped self-interest, greed and ambition. That is the wonderful lesson here—families can work together and resolve issues if you have leadership, values, and an inclusive process. I interviewed Charlie Way, John Darby, Dr. Darby, Berta Way Freeman, and Anne Darby Parker, asking them why the succession from Charlie Way to John Darby worked and what can be learned from their process.

Let's begin with Charlie Way. Charlie was J.C. Long's son-in-law and lawyer, handling all of J.C.'s real estate transactions beginning in 1962. In 1975, Mr. Long became ill and was concerned about dying, although he would live nine more years. He asked Charlie to leave his law practice and come take over J.C. Long and Associates and The Beach Company, the entity that owned the beach property—Isle of Palms. Mr. Long was a classic strong-willed entrepreneur and Charlie was hesitant because he was concerned Mr. Long would continue "to call all the shots" and Charlie would be a figure head.

Charlie had a direct and honest talk with Mr. Long and said he would leave his law practice if and only if Mr. Long gave Charlie complete authority through a general power of attorney. Mr. Long agreed and wrote a letter to all his banks saying that from this day forward Charlie was in charge and that there was only "one Captain of the ship." And to the surprise of many people, Mr. Long complied with and abided by his word to Charlie. According to Charlie, he kept Mr. Long informed and Mr. Long told him after a few years that "Charlie, I only disagreed strongly with what you were doing one time and you were right in doing what you did."

Charlie ran The Beach Company after Mr. Long's death and reported to the two main shareholders, his wife, Mary Ellen, and his sister-in-law, Joyce. Charlie, out of friendship, respect, and good judgment, reached out to Joyce's husband, Dr. Darby, and frequently sought his advice and counsel and they developed a good working relationship that in the 1997 time frame would turn out to be one of the key bedrocks of wisdom and stability, keeping the family focused on the right values.

Charlie never forgot how he came to power and the fact that the strong-willed patriarch, J. C. Long, stated that there can only be one Captain of any ship. By 1997, Charlie had worked in the family business over 25 years building the family's wealth and taking The Beach Company from a small staff to over 200 employees and increasing its asset base geometrically while moving into large commercial developments like Majestic Square while buying, along with Morgan Stanley, Kiawah Island. Charlie was 57 and the Darby family had two sons in the business who were being groomed for the future. Charlie's best advice to family business leaders about succession is:

1. "Begin the successions process while you are healthy so you have a good transition time. Do not wait until you are sick or have to make this big change quickly and too fast for yourself, your successor, and your employees."

2. "Do not underestimate the change—the impact on you—the 'retiree.' Prepare for it in your own mind. It is very different not being Captain of the ship."

3. "You have to educate and promote the change not only internally with employees but also in the community. You have to tell people, 'I am no longer in charge. Ask John.'"

4. "Even though I remained as Chairman, I set clear boundaries and did not attend weekly management meetings or development committee meetings. I did not want people thinking I was looking over John's shoulder."

Charlie, in 1999, made John Darby president and chief operating officer, and in 2003, John became CEO. Charlie's transition out of his role of leader and John's transition into the leader role was eased greatly because Charlie was named by the Governor of South Carolina as the Secretary of Commerce and served from 1999–2002. This gave Charlie something meaningful to move on to and physically required that he be away from Charleston 80 percent of the time. This was not preplanned but was a serendipitous event that made the transition easier. It gave Charlie a big challenge, a big platform to make a contribution.

John Darby was chosen by the family to be the successor while his older brother Buddy continued to concentrate his efforts in Kiawah Island. The family without realizing it applied my Sandbox Theory and decided it was best for the family and Buddy if Buddy became President of Kiawah (a separate entity) and John became president of The Beach Company.

This had two positive impacts. First, neither brother worked or reported to the other; and second, the new structure allowed each brother to lead the business they managed with an entrepreneurial zeal. The result was that Buddy continued his success at Kiawah and John, likewise in five years, more than doubled the size of The Beach Company.

In John Darby's words, his ascension to The Beach Company leadership worked well because:

1. "The succession planning became part and parcel of the 1997 strategic planning process and it occurred over a five-year period which gave everyone time to get used to it. There were no surprises—everyone—me, Charlie and the family were prepared emotionally for the change. Mom and Mary Ellen were in sync and our employees, clients, and lenders had time to adjust."

2. "Charlie and I worked out a working relationship where I, on a weekly basis, would keep him fully briefed and we agreed that any disagreement would never leave our office. We agreed never to contradict or disagree in public."

3. "As importantly, when appropriate, I visited Mary Ellen and Mom— individually the two largest shareholders—briefing them on happenings and getting their input. Remember, they were J. C.'s heirs and the largest shareholders. It was their Company and I acted accordingly."

4. John emphasized, "One thing I want to stress to the readers is that I completely underestimated the change in my and my wife's roles and visibility in the community arising out of my being named CEO. I became a public figure, asked to serve monthly on community boards and when we go out in public, someone always comes up to talk about business or community events. I was not prepared to become a public figure in our community and underestimated the demands the CEO of The Beach Company had."

John succeeded because he came to power humbly. Power did not go to his head. He did not make major changes quickly. He kept his mom, his dad, children, Charlie, and Mary Ellen informed and "in the loop." John had then and continues to have great people skills. He can comfortably relate one on one to a laborer or to the Governor and everyone follows John's mandate of "do what is right for the family—our employees and shareholders."

Under John's leadership, he is preparing the Company for its continued growth by institutionalizing controls, technology, and quality processes. John views his role as that of a steward. "I have to manage the business for the long-term—the fourth generation—those 30 children of my generation of brothers, sisters, and cousins."

Dr. Charles Darby was J.C.'s son-in-law and the father of Buddy and John—the two third-generation shareholders who could have competed against each other to be Charlie's successor. Dr. Darby's role as trusted, wise advisor began with J.C. Long.

When Mr. Long was planning his estate, he talked with Dr. Darby. Dr. Darby advised Mr. Long that the Way family and the Darby family should be 50–50 owners because J.C. "did not want to make five grandchildren feel less loved."

Dr. Darby has this ability to put himself in other's shoes and understand their situation. In talking about family business issues, Dr. Darby wisely stated:

1. "Every family business, to survive and remain harmonious, has to move beyond the strong entrepreneur stage to an open transparent process with outside directors that allows for family shareholders to have meaningful input into how the business is being run."

2. "You have to pay family shareholders not working in the business meaningful dividends, taking into account their age and financial needs. Family shareholders are human—they ask, 'What is in it for me?'"

3. "Family businesses should limit the number of family members employed and any such family employees must have successful prior work experience outside of the Company."

4. "Rotate family board seats to give family shareholders the opportunity to learn about the business and to be heard."

5. "You have to restrict stock transfers in the case of divorce and death to only direct descendents."

I now want to share some thoughts from one of John Darby's sisters and one of his cousins—two young women who have served as Board members under the family shareholder connectedness policies of inclusiveness, input, and transparency. Together they came up with their four key points to keeping a family business successful and having successful successions:

- Tradition;
- Trust;
- Communication; and
- Process

They both talked about the importance of the CEO seeking family input, really listening, and actually valuing the opinions of others. Transparency with the finances and disclosure of all family interactions with the business concerning money was also important. Trust is the lifeblood of keeping a family business successful.

The Way and Darby families have so far worked through successfully many of the common challenges faced by multi-generational family businesses. And they have institutionalized a participatory process and certain values that devalue personal ambition or greed. This is important. It is not only important as to what a family values; it is also important what a family devalues—what is not acceptable behavior. I would advise you to reread and to read often The Beach Company story because it contains many gems of wisdom and sound advice for every family business.

Chapter 13

Choosing a Non-Family Successor CEO

Many times there is no family successor either qualified or willing to become the successor CEO. Then the family is faced with a difficult question: do we sell the business, or do we bring in an outsider to manage our business? And the other question is who will manage the family?

I want to focus on planned successions—those where the current CEO wants to retire in 5–7 years and where for whatever reason, there is no likely family successor. And the family has decided not to sell the business. I want to focus on how you find and choose a non-family member CEO.

The process of finding a successor non-family CEO begins with a needs analysis. What are the likely needs of the business over the next ten years? The business's needs depend upon the age of the business, industry considerations, competitor considerations, life cycle of the products and services and the opportunities for growth. Businesses go through cycles and different personalities and skills are needed at different stages of the business life cycle. For example, different skills and competencies are needed for a fast-paced high growth stage than is needed for a mature plateaued business that is harvesting its returns. When thinking about needs, one also has to take into consideration the family. What events are likely to happen or even could happen in the next ten years that could increase demands on the business for higher financial returns via growth, dividends, or stock liquidity.

Can the business meet those growing financial needs as presently constituted, or is it likely that you need to expand or grow significantly to meet those added demands? If so, what appears to be a stable plateaued business may become an entrepreneurial growth business that requires specific entrepreneurial management skills and competencies. All of this needs to be taken into consideration when creating the profile of a perfect CEO candidate.

A successor CEO profile must also include the skills needed to communicate, educate, and deal with family shareholders. One cannot underestimate this skill. The fact is that the new CEO will work for the family and must earn the respect and trust of the family. Working for a family—being CEO of a family business is very different than working for an institution or public company. Families disagree and family issues intrude on the business and family issues will influence business discussions. Sometimes the family will make decisions based on family needs or issues that could differ from the decision made solely on business considerations.

Most outside family CEOs underestimate the time, the patience, and the work needed to keep the family informed, educated, and relatively happy. Non-family CEOs are surprised that family members may recruit them as aides or support for a particular position in a family disagreement. By definition, CEOs taking stands on what is the right business decision will sometimes disagree or go against some family member. Non-family CEOs have to be comfortable with this added complexity, and comfortable that he or she will not get their way all the time.

Non-family CEOs can never forget:

- They are *not* family; and
- They *serve* at the discretion of the family

My experience is that it takes a special type of person and personality to be a non-family CEO of a family-owned business. What types of people should you be concerned about? True entrepreneurs, strong personalities, egocentric, impatient, very ambitious, very greedy, or poor listeners are high-risk hires for any family.

One of the best non-family CEOs I have ever worked with was a former CPA with a major national accounting firm. The family business was a client of his for ten years before he was hired by the family and worked another ten years in the business on business and family financial matters. He had high standards, the highest integrity, and earned the trust and respect of the family. He never lost sight that in whatever position he served, he served at the will of the family.

He maintained his independence—never participated in or favored a family branch or allowed himself to be used by a family member for political purposes. He made sure his positions on issues were known to all of the family and he knew how to listen, educate, and disagree in a manner that did not offend people. He was not a "yes man" but he did not get his ego heavily invested in a business decision because all he could do was make recommendations to the family. He spent time with each family member—heard them out, communicated often—and placed great emphasis on making sure the owners were well informed.

Once you have created the profile of your "perfect CEO" and, as importantly, the types of people or personalities you should avoid, you should prioritize or rank the requirements. In all cases, you lessen the risk or probability of a mistake in choosing a non-family CEO if, as part of the profile, you require that all candidates have deep industry or business experience in your type of business. And to further lessen your risk, you should first seek candidates that have either worked in your business or have worked with or for your business in some capacity for some meaningful time. The key here is to consider candidates with industry experience, and people with whom you have had extensive experience either as a customer, a supplier, a competitor, or as a service provider. *If possible, hire someone you know.*

Once you have made up a list of candidates from within and from outside the company, you then have to create an interview process during which you, key employees, and key family members spend time getting to know the candidates. Do background checks, reference checks, and personal interviews with people who have worked with and for each candidates.

With the candidate's written permission, look at credit reports and have someone check for lawsuits, tax liens, criminal and traffic incidents. Watch out for employee sex, age, race, harassment claims. Watch out for gambling debts, excessive leverage, and high profile lifestyles. Have each candidate take standardized personality profiles and values assessment tests. And understand it is very hard to find out the truth or the true nature of people in today's litigious society by personal reference checks. Do everything you can to check out your candidates. Then you have to assess each candidate against your need profile and make a judgment.

By starting this succession process at least three years (but five years is better) ahead of your planned retirement, you have time to train, educate, and evaluate your choice. So in most cases, your potential successor should not be hired as the CEO. No, he or she should come into the company with the expectation that if he or she performs at the highest levels and standards, he or she would be the likely next CEO, but there are no guarantees of that result.

You need a trial period—time to see if you made the right choice. And if not, you need time to try another candidate. I have had clients who made the right choice the first time following this process. And I have had clients have to make three choices before finding the right person. Starting early gives you time to test and time to correct mistakes. And correct your mistakes quickly.

Let us assume you made the right choice for the successor CEO. Some other common issues are:

- Should the new non-family CEO also become chairman of the board?
- Should the new non-family CEO be given stock options or stock ownership?

- Should the new CEO be made a member of the Board of Directors?
- Should the new CEO sign a contract and a non-compete agreement?

I recommend that when you appoint a non-family CEO, you detach, or split, or bifurcate the CEO and the chairman roles and positions. The non-family CEOs primary job is to manage the business. The chairman of the board should be the senior family leader whose job is to oversee the CEO, manage the board and to manage the family issues revolving around or involving the business.

The chairman should be the de facto Chief Family Officer. Thus, the chairman not only should possess wisdom, maturity, judgment, integrity, and emotional intelligence but must also have the trust and respect of the family and be willing to work hard educating, communicating with, and listening to family members. He and she must, through his or her actions, execute on the family goals of inclusion, input, and consensus building as well as be a role model for and represent the family's values. This is much more than a ceremonial or titular position in multi-generational, successful family businesses. It should be a paying job with an annual salary commensurate with the time and expertise. The chairman's role is not to operate the business on a daily basis; the chairman's role is to oversee management, manage the board, and the family. The bigger the business, the bigger the family, the more important this position becomes. Most of my clients view this position as such when they have a non-family CEO and compensate the chairman anywhere from $100,000 to $250,000 annually.

Should the new non-family CEO be given stock options or stock ownership in the business? No. Family businesses should be owned by family. This does not mean that you should not fairly reward the CEO for value created and outstanding performance. I am a big believer in phantom stock plans that allow senior employees to earn the financial benefits of stock ownership without technically and legally becoming shareholders. And I am a big believer in vesting programs that vest such benefits over a five-year period for each year of the grants. You want your CEO to be aligned with the best long-term interests of the business and family—not short-term. You do not want business decisions being made primarily to boost short-term earnings in order to pay big bonuses. No—you are looking for long-term, consistent, high performance.

Not all of my clients have agreed with me on this issue. I have one client who has granted stock options to its five senior managers that vest over five years. And if a manager leaves the company for a competitor, their vested options are cashed out and the unvested options expire. When those managers retire, they can remain shareholders (against my advice) and the stock can pass on to their heirs, which will result in the family company having non-family shareholders.

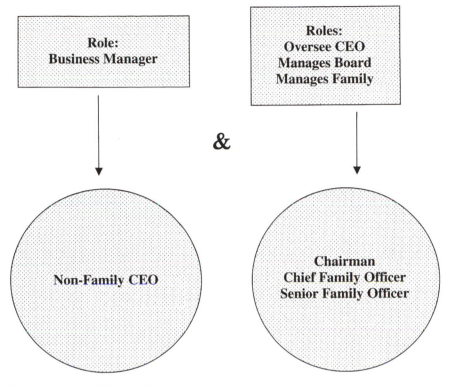

Figure 13.1. Different Roles

Should the non-family CEO become a member of the Board of Directors? Yes. Serving on the Board exposes more of the family to the CEO on a quarterly basis and likewise exposes the CEO to the family and their values, concerns, and issues. Such two-way communications should help build trust and respect and sensitize the non-family CEO to the impact of family needs upon the business.

Should the non-family CEO have an employment contract and a non-compete clause? YES. You should seek legal advice on the enforceability, geographical scope, and timeframe of non-compete clauses but the last thing you want is your CEO leaving, taking employees and customers and starting a competitive business. Your business should not be a training ground for future competitors.

The next stage of the process is the transitioning in of the new CEO and the transitioning out of the retiring CEO. Because of the test period you have gone through over a substantial time period, the new CEO should have learned all aspects of the business and earned the trust and respect of the employees and customers and of the family.

When the new non-family CEO takes over the CEO position, he or she and the retiring CEO will be tested by employees who will try to go around the new CEO to the old CEO and have decisions reversed or modified if the new CEO makes changes. It is *imperative* that the old CEO not interfere or undermine the new CEO, and it is imperative that the new CEO take his or her time in making changes and be patient and allow the organization to digest any change. Making several major structural, strategic, or personnel changes quickly is a recipe for disaster.

The new CEO should have had discussions with the old CEO and the board and have sought their input and consensus on what changes need to be made, when they should be made, and how they should be made. I want to share with you the details and story of a very successful family business transition to a non-family CEO. This is a case of masterful management of the transition by the retiring second generation chairman and CEO and the use of new power by the incoming CEO.

Chapter 14

Case Study: Edens & Avant

Building a successful sustainable business is hard. Keeping it prosperous and being able to manage the transition of that business to the next generation of owners is even harder.

Edens & Avant is a remarkable company. I have worked with this company since 1995. Joe Edens, the founder, visionary, and patriarch, is a rare entrepreneur—a man who knows his strengths and weaknesses, understands people, and is able to confront reality and proactively manage change. Although Joe did not finish college, he is wise and learned. He has spent his life driven to succeed, but to succeed in the right way with the right values.

In 2002 at age 61, Joe brought in an outsider to take over as CEO of his company in order to position the company for the future. The purpose of this chapter is to share with you how Joe Edens planned and proactively managed his succession process. But, as importantly the Edens family business history is rich with a heritage of Joe's grandfather and father both having built successful businesses and significant wealth both of which were lost and not passed on to future family generations. Joe Edens' values and approach to succession planning and legacy planning were all colored by the prior generations' experiences creating and losing significant wealth during their lifetimes.

The Edens' succession story is the result of three dynamics:

1. The strong desire of Joe Edens not to lose his family's fortune, as his father and grandfather did;

2. The dramatic changes occurring in the shopping center industry because of consolidation and changing capital markets; and

3. The change in the management skill sets needed to lead the next generation of real estate companies.

First, what is Edens & Avant? Edens & Avant is the largest private owner of neighborhood community retail shopping centers in the United States. It owns 163 shopping centers comprising 19 million square feet. Edens & Avant employs over 175 people and has net operating income of $160 million. Edens & Avant's business is valued at approximately $2.5 billion. It is based in Columbia, South Carolina, and today is owned primarily by the Edens family, management, and three institutional investors.

Its operations extend geographically from New England to Florida with major regional offices in Boston, Washington, DC, and Atlanta, Georgia. Edens is a full service real estate development and management company involved in the design, construction, leasing, management, asset management, rehabilitation, and financing of retail and retail mixed-use properties.

Edens' dominance and success in the retail center industry dates back to 1929 when Joe Edens' father, Joe Edens, Sr., along with his older brother, Drake opened a fresh produce stand on Assembly Street across from The Farmers Market in Columbia.

Joe, Sr. was one of 16 children born to a self-made wealthy cotton farmer. Joe, Sr.'s father was an entrepreneur and even though he was rich as a cotton farmer, he wanted to move into more profitable farming of peaches. Unfortunately, before he was able to transition his crop he lost his fortune because of the boll weevil disaster that wiped out his cotton crops. Joe, Sr.'s father died in despair and grief having lost his family's livelihood and fortune. When Joe, Sr. was ten years old, the time of his father's death, he dropped out of school to work to help support the family. He never returned to formal schooling, but continued to learn through self-teaching and the "school of hard knocks."

In 1929 at the age of 17, Joe, Sr. and his brother, Drake, opened their first produce stand. Using their $200 of capital, they bought an expensive Toledo hanging scale and their first batch of produce from wholesalers.

Joe, Sr. spoke about the risk and fragility of the start-up in a speech he gave in 1954:

> In the late twenties, with two hundred dollars ($200), a barrel of apples, and faith in God, my brother and I opened a small fruit store on Assembly Street in Columbia. Dealing only in fruits and vegetables and without any refrigeration, selling was our business from the very beginning. From the orchard in the mountains of Virginia, my brother, Drake, bought five carloads of apples, one car to be shipped each week for a period of five weeks. Early on the first day of the week we were notified by the freight agent that we had five cars of apples on hand for our account. Need I say that someone had made an awful mistake. With concerted effort we began selling apples in dozens, bushels, pecks, and in every other conceivable fashion. In nine days we were successful in selling four carloads, and without

question every home in Columbia had an ample supply of apples for the winter. Of course we had sold the best first, including Delicious, Winsap, and other choice varieties. The last was a carload of Pippins, the little greenish looking apple that in those days no one wanted. All of a sudden the weather turned warm. Realizing that Columbia was well-stocked we began to try our luck in other towns, including Winnsboro, Chester, Great Falls, and others. After trying for two days the customers I called on had all but convinced me that the product I was selling was no good and would not sell at any price. In fact, I began to wonder if the apples were poisoned. I never shall forget as I returned to Columbia late Friday afternoon after a final try in Augusta, Georgia. The apples had become spotted and in an old house near the freight station where the remainder of this car had been stored, the bees had begun to swarm all over the fruit. We were discouraged, and almost defeated but we knew that we must sell this last car that was the profit on the five cars, if we were to remain in business. From greater powers, the solution to our problem came to us. By telegram we ordered a cider press from Atlanta, Georgia, and by late Saturday night our precious cargo had been converted into cider—in fact, honey flavored cider, something new in the day. On Monday morning I went back over the same route where I had tried to sell the apples. Packed six gallons to the case, I sold every case in one day without any trouble; and realized by far more than the apples would have brought at top price.

The Edens fruit stand diversified when its customers requested non-perishable items like flour and canned sardines. In 1931, they moved to a bigger store of 3000 square feet. In 1932, they expanded and opened a second store in Columbia. And by 1950, they were opening 10,000 square-foot stores. Over the time period from 1932 to 1956, they continued to expand in South Carolina opening 36 more stores for a total of 38 stores.

From a small fruit stand in 1929 over a 25-year period, Edens Food Stores built a bakery, a huge warehouse and acquired its own fleet of refrigerated trailer trucks. Sales grew from a little over $3 million in 1945 to over $16 million in 1956. Edens Foods was a dominant grocer in South Carolina. The Edens brothers created a culture based on "That There May Be More For All" and they believed employees were part of the family all dedicated to "friendly and courteous service."

The culture of Edens Foods where Joe, Jr. started working at age 8 was evidenced by Edens Employees 1000% Club. Like many family businesses, Joe Edens, Sr.'s personal values became the family business' core values and these were the values that our main actor, Joe, Jr., learned working in the business and at home.

Edens Food Stores

Looking	1947	Forward
LOYALTY		100%
INTEREST		100%
DEPENDABILITY		100%
RELIABILITY		100%
ENERGY		100%
ABILITY		100%
CHARACTER		100%
COOPERATION		100%
SALESMANSHIP		100%
EFFICIENCY		100%
TOTAL		1000%

"Let's Make It 1000% for '47"

In 1956, Joe, Sr. and his brother, Drake, merged Edens Foods with Winn Lovett—a Jacksonville, Florida, grocery chain that became the modern Winn Dixie. The two brothers received approximately $12 million in stock that in 1956 was a substantial sum of money. Winn Lovett set up a division in Columbia called Edens Winn Lovett that became Edens Winn Dixie, after merging with Dixie Homestore Food Chain headquartered in Greenville, South Carolina, in late 1956 and ultimately Winn Dixie. Winn Dixie wanted Joe, Sr. to move to Jacksonville, Florida and to enter top management but his family said no.

So Joe, Sr. at the age of 44 was a multi-millionaire and left Winn Dixie to enter politics and public service with the local hospital and the Methodist Church, becoming a trustee of both Emory University and Woffard College and political contemporary of Governor Strom Thurmond. In addition, Joe, Sr. was the driving force behind the changing of the form of city government in Columbia, South Carolina from a mayoral concentrated power to a distributed power structured with a City Council and City Manager. Joe, Sr. was constantly asked to head fund raising campaigns for local hospitals, churches, the YMCA, and other organizations.

Joe, Sr. missed the business world. He went looking for a new business opportunity. And he found one—a manufacturing business that custom made architectural plastics and aluminum products. Aluminum and plastics were hot "new" products—they did not rust—that was very important in the wet, humid South and they did not have to be repainted often like wood.

From 1957–1967, the new business moved from one crisis to another. As Joe, Jr. stated, "the business went from one chaos to another—this business did not play to dad's strengths. He was a terrific food retailer, but he was completely lost in the world of manufacturing." By age 55, ten years after buying the manufacturing business, Joe, Sr. had depleted and exhausted the millions he had made in the food business. Like his father, Joe, Sr. had become a very wealthy man at an early age and like his father, he had lost the family fortune.

With a heritage of individuality, entrepreneurship, risk-taking, not being satisfied with great success, Joe, Jr.—our main character in this wonderful story—was born in 1941. Joe, Jr.'s working life began at age 8 in his father's food stores bagging groceries.

Joe, Jr. (hereafter referred to as "Joe") worked 20 hours a week—three hours after school on Thursdays, 4½ hours after school on Fridays, and 12½ hours on Saturdays for a weekly paycheck of $4.65. Joe learned business very early in his life. In order to maximize his earnings, he frequently would carry groceries home for ladies or to their cars. Joe stated two fundamental business principles about customers that he learned early in his life bagging groceries:

- Your tips will be bigger if you are nice to the customers.
- You make the most money if you learn which customers are the big tippers and which ones appreciate your prompt, competent, and courteous service.

Joe worked in the food stores all through elementary and high school and worked full-time six days a week in the summer. Joe was promoted from bagger and merchandise refiller to meat cutter at age 12. Joe learned the food business and retail from the ground up. His daddy's admonitions about service, courtesy, friendliness, and quality were all taken in along with his family's strong Methodist beliefs and he always espoused the principle of "doing unto others as you would have them do unto you." Those values would drive Joe not only to success but to being a cutting edge innovator in the real estate industry and to build the foundation of one of the biggest private real estate companies in the United States, now with over $2.5 billion of assets.

It is this journey that is interesting because the lineage of two lost entrepreneurial family fortunes, both built from meager beginnings, set the stages for how Joe would face his issues of "How much financial success is enough?" and "Will I know when to get out?"

Joe was not an "A" student in high school but he was a great football player. Joe played on both offense and defense as the offensive center and defensive nose guard and was scouted by 35 colleges and universities. In small Southern towns, football was and still is a dominant means of recognition and the pride of the town. Joe's team in his senior year won the state championship, the only time Columbia High School has ever done that.

But in winning the State Championship, Joe suffered an ankle injury in the closing minutes of the game that ended not only his career but also his way to leave Columbia and choose his own college and way into the world.

Joe left high school having earned the honors of "Best All Around Student," "Friendliest Student," and as Captain of the football team. Even with his success and personality, his father thought he needed more discipline and wanted Joe to attend college at the Citadel, and receive military discipline.

Joe attended the Citadel and as in high school, Joe did not shine academically. Although Joe loved the military aspects of the school and because of his leadership successes in high school, he set a goal of becoming the Regimental Student Commander—the top ranked student military position. But with his mediocre grades, his goal was out of his reach. At this time, his father's venture into the custom manufacturing business had begun to "sink" the family both financially and emotionally. Joe was made to feel that he was a financial burden being at the Citadel, especially since he would no longer be qualified to be Regimental Commander. So, at age 20, Joe quit college and came home with a heavy guilt load.

Joe's father was hard on him, berating him for his failure. In some ways, one wonders whether Joe became an outlet for his father's fears and guilt of falling from being one of the town's financial, political, and charitable leaders to a financially and emotionally broken man.

So at age 20, Joe Edens needed to earn some money and he went to the want ads in the Columbia newspaper. He answered an ad for "Real Estate Salesman Wanted—No College Degree Necessary"—not because he liked real estate and because he was qualified, but because he had no college degree.

Joe went to work for Boineau Realty selling residential and some commercial real estate. Joe worked for Boineau for one year and in 1961 his father's Sales Manager recruited Joe to come to work in sales in his father's business reporting to the Sales Manager—not his father. After 18 months, Joe was elevated to Sales Manager due to his selling success.

Joe felt a duty to help his dad and spent the next five years of his life trying to make his father's business work. In 1966, Joe and his daddy had a big blow-up and falling out. Joe hated the manufacturing business but did his duty. In 1966, Joe left the business. From age 20 to 26, Joe basically was doing his family's duty and trying to earn his daddy's respect and love. Joe's daddy was a proponent of "tough love."

While Joe worked in the manufacturing business, his hobby was buying old houses and fixing them up as rental units primarily with 100 percent financing. During the time period 1961–1966, Joe had accumulated over 300 rental units. All of the equity created and income derived from these homes was given by Joe to his daddy.

The ambition and drive in Joe Edens was strong. He opened a sole proprietorship, Joe Edens Realty, with $500 of capital that could be drawn down on a Banker's Trust credit card. Joe bought some used furniture and rented an office for $225 a month. Unfortunately, Joe's father's health and financial condition continued to deteriorate. His cousin approached him and said he would support Joe if Joe would return and operate his father's business while it was sold or liquidated.

Joe agreed to help if his Daddy would agree. He did and Joe left his new real estate business. Joe's father's business was sold ten months later and Joe immediately returned to his new sole proprietorship with no more capital than he had to begin with.

In the latter part of 1966, a serendipitous event occurred that changed Joe Edens' personal life and business life. Remembering that Joe grew up in the grocery business and loved it, he heard that a new food chain from Greenville called Bi-Lo wanted to expand to Columbia.

Joe, without an appointment, immediately drove to Greenville in an attempt to see the CEO of Bi-Lo (Mr. Frank Outlaw) in order to sell him a site for a grocery store in Columbia. Joe got to the Bi-Lo warehouse and gave the secretary his card and told her about Edens Food Stores and asked if Mr. Outlaw could give him five minutes. Mr. Outlaw was a former executive with the Dixie Homestore Chain, which merged with Edens Winn Lovett in late 1956. Joe Edens left Greenville with a 30-day exclusive to find Bi-Lo its first Columbia site. Joe found what he thought would be a great site—an existing mobile home park and four adjoining style family homes. What Bi-Lo said next was critical. They told Joe they did not want to own a site, but rather they wanted Joe to build a shopping center and to lease them their store. They wanted him to be their developer and landlord, not their site procurement agent. And thus, a new business direction was set for Joe.

Shopping centers were starting to evolve in the mid-1960s. Grocery and drug stores wanted to reach new customers in neighborhoods. At that time in Columbia, there were only three neighborhood centers and they were built in the late 1950s. Joe Edens in 1967 built his first shopping center that was a 75,000 square-foot center with a Bi-Lo food store, drug store, shoe store, Dollar Store, and dry cleaners. The shopping center was named Edens Plaza, which by the way, the Edens children still own today.

Edens Plaza became the birthright ultimately of Edens & Avant, the largest private owner of grocery-anchored neighborhood real estate centers in the United States, all begun by an entrepreneur's unannounced "cold call" on the president of Bi-Lo Groceries.

Joe Edens' story is interesting not only because it is a story of entrepreneurship, family fortunes made and lost, but also because Joe Edens' 30-year story from 1967 to 1997 when he brought in institutional capital to reduce his leverage burden and to provide substantial equity growth capital is who the story of the growth of an industry and the story of the vicissitudes of commercial real estate financing cycles and pendulum swings.

To build real estate, you need capital and lots of it. And that capital needs to be patient because it takes time to build and to stabilize commercial developments.

Joe's 30-year career was a huge success but it was not easy because of the velocity of and the wide surges in interest rates and capital sources. Joe Edens lived through and built his fortune in spite of 21 percent interest rates and the mortgage REIT and bank debacle of the late 1960s and early 1970s; in spite of the 1970s syndication craze and its demise in the early 1980s; in spite of the savings and loan busts of the mid 1980s and in spite of the real estate depression that began in the late 1980s and lasted until the public REIT revival in 1992.

Throughout this time period, you had continuous changes in the sources of real estate capital and the structuring of deals. The players kept changing and how deals were financed kept changing and to survive in a capital intensive business, you had to be flexible, creative, and determined. And Joe almost went under three times. But he did not. He refused to suffer the same fate that befell both his father and grandfather.

From his first shopping center development in 1967 at age 26, Joe continued to construct and lease shopping centers through the 1970s, hiring a few employees. But Joe was fixated with trying to figure out how to manage the risk of real estate created by high interest rates, changing financing sources, and more competition.

Joe did not live "high." Whatever net cash he derived from the shopping centers was reinvested in the business. Nonetheless, Joe wanted a way to smooth out financially the ups and downs or volatility of real estate development. Joe learned as a child the benefits of monthly dividend income. He, as a bag boy, bought Edens Food stock that became Winn Dixie stock that paid monthly dividends. Based on this childhood experience, he changed the payout on leasing commissions from being paid in a lump sum up front to being paid monthly during the term lease.

But even more importantly, Joe began thinking about building a full service real estate company with third-party brokerage, leasing, and management in order to have a more reliable source of predictable monthly cash flow.

The volatility of the real estate business impacted Joe greatly—probably because of what happened to his father financially. Joe, as well as being thin on working capital, was so concerned about losing everything that he and his now wife of over 35 years dated for over five years before getting married. He credits her patience and unwavering support in helping him overcome many business challenges and obstacles.

He set a goal of making $3 million by the time he was 34 years of age. Joe reached his goal when he was 33. He had planned to retire and spend the vast majority of his time on charitable and philanthropic work. However, Joe came to the conclusion that at age 33 it was not in his persona to retire and that he could do more for more many people by continuing to do what he loved—real estate—and he set a new goal to expand his business to be the first regional full-service real estate company based in Columbia, South Carolina. And he did.

By the mid-1970s, Joe had built 38 shopping centers and had equity in those centers of over $3 million. His ambition was fueled by the desire to build a regional full service real estate company. This led him to merge in 1979 with a leading brokerage firm, McTeer & Company, to form Edens & McTeer, Inc. Edens & McTeer was a success growing along every dimension—doubling its business activity in three years to over $125 million and more than doubling its managed projects, square footage of new leasers, and reaching a construction start of new shopping centers of one per month.

By 1982, Edens owned 64 shopping centers in Alabama, Georgia, Mississippi, North Carolina, and South Carolina, and eight office buildings in Columbia, South Carolina. In July 1982, Joe brought Dan Avant in as a Principal and changed the name of the company to Edens and Avant, its current name. What drove Joe Edens? His answers are interesting:

> I was driven to be successful financially because being well-off put you in a position to do things for your family and for others. When Daddy was in the food business, he would take us with him to New York City when he visited suppliers and we went to Broadway plays, ate at the Stork Club and it gave us broadening experiences. And when he sold to Winn Dixie, he dedicated himself to education and hospital fund raising until his new business consumed him.

From 1978 to 1986, Joe took advantage of the opportunities to liquefy a significant amount of his net worth and removed enough money from the business and placed it into family trusts so that finally after nearly 20 years of volatility and change in the real estate capital markets, the Edens Family had wealth that could survive into the next generation—unlike the unfortunate business investments made by Joe's father and the boll weevil disaster that destroyed his grandfather's wealth.

While Joe was building his real estate company, in addition, he was very active in community service, philanthropic work, and politics. For example, at age 27, Joe began serving on the Columbia Board of the National Bank of South Carolina. At age 29, he became chairman of the board of the Republic National Bank because he had been successful in a proxy fight to unseat the existing Board. He brought in new directors and new management that resulted in the financial recovery and tripling of the share price of the bank. Joe did this at the request of his cousin, the same cousin that had helped Joe's daddy in his business. After selling Republic National Bank, Joe, at age 37, was asked to join the Board of C & S Bank of South Carolina, the second largest bank holding company in South Carolina.

Joe served as a member of the Board of Visitors of the Medical University of South Carolina and was appointed by two Governors to the Boards of the State of South Carolina Parks, Recreation, and Tourism Commission and to the State of South Carolina Natural Resources Commission. Joe also served as a Trustee of the Hammond School, Chairman of the City of Columbia Development Corporation and like his father, has been actively involved in raising funds for many Columbia charities.

All of this is important because Joe had made a personal promise to give back to the community and to help others. Joe's success was not selfish—he was raised to help others. As Joe stated, "I was never motivated to be the richest person in town; I was motivated to make a difference."

During the 1980s, Joe participated and helped create state of the art real estate financing structures with Balcor and with WestPac Investors Trust of California. These innovations are known today as wrap-mortgage financings, as well as collateralization of loans secured by groups of first and second mortgages. Today they are commonly done on Wall Street in the CMB market.

He also expanded in the 1980s to suburban office, apartment complexes, light industrial, and built one of the largest class A high rise office building, a 320,000 square-foot Bank of America Plaza that opened in 1989 in Columbia.

Joe's forage into real estate product diversification, while successful, exposed him to big risks and he found it hard to contain and control costs of those projects and he refocused again on what he knew best—grocery-anchored retail centers.

And then, the real estate depression of the 1989–1992 time period hit the industry and Joe very hard. The traditional bank lenders withdrew from the markets voluntarily or because of changes resulting from mergers of local banks into major bank holding companies. The savings and loan scandals crippled that industry and that source of capital. Joe had to spend over 80 percent of his time scrambling to find new capital. And Joe did find a new lender and create a new financing structure with Protective Life Insurance Company of Birmingham, Alabama. Joe financed $170 million with Protective.

Liquidity started to return to the real estate markets in 1993 through the public debt securitization marketplace that arose out of the savings and loans bailouts and by the re-emergence of the public REIT marketplace that began in the late fall of 1993 and burgeoned until August 1994. Some of Joe's competitors had accessed patient private equity sources and one competitor was going public.

Joe knew his strengths. Yet, he also was realistic about his and his company's weaknesses. He did not have the management depth to go public and Joe knew he did not have the temperament to be a public company CEO. By 1995, Joe was 54 years old. In his words, "My war horse years were behind me. But I had to do something to find long-term capitalization for the business and for my employees."

Joe had to partner with a strong financial player "who could get along with his cornbread, collard greens, black-eye peas group."

Joe, throughout his career, had some unique skills for an entrepreneur. He had the uncanny ability to assess reality, to face the facts and proactively take action. Joe "never drank the entrepreneurial Kool-aid" of being invincible and all-knowing.

Remember, he came from an entrepreneurial heritage of losing fortunes. That experience made Joe obsessed with not losing what he had made. What helped Joe throughout his career was this ability to face reality and the knowledge that no matter how well you did—how hard you worked, outside factors could take it all from you—whether that was the boll weevil or the fickle real estate financing markets.

And it is that knowledge that even motivates Joe today when he, as a director of the Federal Reserve Bank of Richmond, presses for programs to help displaced Southern manufacturing employees who have lost their jobs because of cheaper labor costs in the developing world. Joe's position also allows him to insert real-time information on real estate trends, the impacts of events on retailers, and the resulting impact on consumers into the top levels of government decision-making on monetary policy.

Upon reflection, Joe looks back on a 37-year career humbly and believes it was the loyalty of his wife, children, friends, employees, his lenders, and other business associates that kept him in the game. And he thinks people were loyal to him because he was "sincere in his actions and deeds."

"Many people helped me who had no obligation to do so." Joe's humility is further evidenced by his discomfort with accolades and the fact that he has helped many people and many charities anonymously.

In 1997, Joe entered into the first of three major transactions where he sold part of his company to the State of Michigan Retirement Systems for $150 million. Joe knew that for his company to compete against the new public companies, he had to institutionalize and recapitalize the company with long-term money. He believed his industry would undergo major changes driven by technology, grocery chain consolidation, and new retail formats, trends, and players.

When Joe finalized the Michigan deal in 1997, Joe was 56 years old and he had no readily available successor. Joe's oldest son, Joe III, worked in the business and was a superb construction professional but he had no experience in the capital markets—which really drove the business. Joe had built a company with over 150 employees who were part of his family and he tried to instill family pride and caring throughout his company.

"I tried to instill in these people that they care about each other and be there for each other when illness, death, or financial troubles arise. I tried to teach them that they can be better and if I critique them, it's because I care about them and want them to be better."

Joe started thinking about finding his successor. "I knew I needed someone with a different skillset, different energy level but who would appreciate our culture and our family." Joe wanted somebody who "was grounded and humble"—not an arrogant or totally "what's-in-it-for-me" person. Joe wanted someone who "truly believed that all people at all levels in the company are important. Most people coming to work want to do good. A leader's job is to help them do that."

"I wanted somebody who would truly be color blind and gender blind— somebody who would have the passion and drive to make this company the best in the industry."

Joe thought a lot about what successor qualifications were important to him—what skills or competencies the changing industry would demand. What skills did the company not have? But most important of all was the "heart and soul" of the person. Would he treat people with dignity, honestly, and do what he or she said? Accordingly to Joe, "Values are not just to be talked about but also acted on with deeds."

Joe reflected on how and why he "made it." In his mind, he had no money, no education, no training and "was not the brightest penny in the purse." He attributed all his success to two things:

- How he dealt with people—with sincerity, honesty and caring; and
- Doing what he said he would do.

Joe had two of his three children working in the company—Joe and Kim. But he was comfortable that they would be all right because he required both to prove themselves and work somewhere else before joining the company. That way they would have self-confidence and know they could succeed on their own. And when they joined the company, he did not want them reporting to himself nor working with or for him.

In 2000, Joe started thinking seriously about outside candidates from the banking world, from investment banking and from competitors. He began discussions with a couple of people in 2001. As Joe contemplated his successor, his motivations were two-fold:

- Try to position his company to survive and compete in the next round of real estate changes; and

- Do what was best for his family, his employees, and himself—in that order.

Joe's analysis or thought process was instructive. He thought a lot about how his industry had and would continue to change. He created a checklist of skills he thought the next CEO would need. And he thought even more about values—how he wanted his company run.

During all of this, Joe spent time at his personal refuge—his farm—at the kitchen table with his beloved loyal dog Chris at his feet. Joe reflected on his Daddy and came to peace with his Daddy's "tuff love" and "learned to love the good parts of Daddy and let the bad go." And Joe thought about his aunt who was now in her 90s and about her life. She was single and one of the most successful, independent businesswomen in the state. Having been chairman of the county council, chairman of the Richland Memorial, the largest hospital system in South Carolina, chairman of the National PBS, she enrolled in college at age 73—the college where she had served as chairman of the board of trustees for many years—and got her degree at age 75. Today she walks three miles every morning to her table at the Columbia Capitol City Club where she pays 99 cents for the breakfast buffet.

Joe was coming to grips with his background and his own legacy and what he wanted to pass on to his 300 employees. Joe's children were young. In 2000, during this time of reflection Michael was 26, Kim was 28, and Joe III was 36. Joe knew "my twilight is here."

Joe began earnest discussions in March 2001 with Terry Brown, an investment banker whom he first met in 1996 when he hired Terry as advisor on the restructuring of his Company and the capital infusion from the State of Michigan. Terry was a graduate of the University of Georgia and had spent his entire career at Arthur Andersen, first as a tax accountant and then was the second employee of Andersen Corporate Finance, a specialty practice within Arthur Andersen of which he ultimately became CEO of its North American Operations.

Terry was raised in a small town in Georgia—Elberton, and his mother was a homemaker and his father was a former U.S. Army man and U.S. Postal Service employee having served for years as Elberton Postmaster. Terry had married his high school sweetheart, Lisa, and they had three children.

Joe reflected that he "intuitively trusted Terry the first time he met him." Over the period from 1996 until Terry joined Edens and Avant in May 2002 as the new CEO, Terry and Joe talked three or four times a week about the business and its needs.

When Joe raised the issue in 2001, he "had never hired a successor before—never dealt with the issue and I had no place to go for advice."

Terry was not enthusiastic about leaving his position at Andersen nor about leaving Atlanta for the smaller city of Columbia. Terry was concerned about opportunities for his three sons. Joe spent the summer and fall of 2001 talking to Terry but little progress was made. Terry's concern and his focus on his family only emphasized to Joe that Terry had good core values and he was not seeking a CEO job for prestige, status, or ego gratification.

Joe had "tested" Terry for years while working together and Terry knew the company and its key people very well. Joe had talked about Terry's possibility of coming to Edens and Avant with his wife, children, and the top people in his Company. Joe had one senior executive who was hopeful she would be qualified to be the next CEO.

Around late October 2001, Joe told Terry, "I need to move on this so if you are interested, we need to make some progress." Terry thought about it and said that he and his family would come to Columbia after Christmas to explore housing, schools, and the community.

Joe's initial thoughts were to bring Terry in as the CFO for a year and then transition him to CEO. Terry rejected that overture and told Joe that if he came—it had to be as CEO. Joe stepped back and continued to think about this process. Was he ready to turn over his company that he built up from a $500 to a $1.5 billion company? Was he willing to give up decision-making after 35 years of being the chief decision maker? Underlying Joe's thought process was the fact that he "felt comfortable that Terry valued the things that were important to me."

Although Joe did not think about it this way, while he was talking with Terry he began preparing all of the different constituencies for the change and to get their buy-in. Joe managed this process of disclosure, communication, discussion and input masterfully, with the following:

- Mrs. Edens;
- His three children;
- Key employees;
- Board of Directors; and
- Key company institutional investors.

Did Joe have second thoughts in early 2002 as he and Terry negotiated? Joe, in his own words, "did not want to be like Michael Jordan and not know when to call it quits." Joe "did not want to be somebody who could not turn loose."

But what is instructive about Joe and his process for other family businesses is that not only did Joe focus on:

- The skills a successor should possess;
- The values a successor should have; and
- The experience and knowledge the successor has about the company.

But Joe also proactively managed the change process by:

- Communicating and getting buy-in from all affected stakeholders; and
- Creating a transition process that was "set up for success and support for the new CEO" because Joe, more than anyone, knew that the succession HAD to work.

In thinking about this transition process for months, Joe focused on the granular details of dailyness—what and how he would act once the new CEO arrived—down to Joe requiring that the new CEO move into Joe's office.

In early 2002 Terry told Joe he was ready to negotiate a deal but he had one major concern—Joe's loyal senior employee who thought she should be Joe's successor. In response to Terry concerns, Joe set up a face-to-face meeting in Columbia amongst the three of them and the issue as to whether the employee would work for Terry as the new CEO was discussed openly and bluntly. The answer was yes.

Joe then did something that was brilliant and a technique that I have copied and advised other families to use in hiring key executives or choosing a chairman of the board. Joe asked Terry to submit in writing a short memo "stating why he was the right person to become CEO of Edens & Avant" and to write about what he felt about the opportunity.

Another important action Joe took was to ask two independent directors to negotiate Terry's compensation package. Joe intentionally removed the difficult issues of how much money and stock ownership from his and Terry's day-to-day talks in March of 2001. Again, remember Joe knew that this had to work and Joe told his compensation committee that Terry should be paid at market rates and he should have stock ownership on day one—he had to be an owner of the business he was running. To accomplish all of this, Joe voluntarily surrendered, for the best interests of the company, stock options, vested restricted stock and took a salary reduction so that the board would not have to deal with these things as issues in considering Terry's compensation package.

The deal was finalized and Joe moved to transition planning including:

- Joe moving his office;
- How Joe would announce to the Company the new CEO;
- What Joe would do to show people internally and as importantly, externally that Terry was in charge;
- Setting up meetings with the company's key bankers and tenants to introduce Terry; and
- Setting up meetings with the leaders in Columbia, South Carolina introducing Terry to the community.

When Terry came to work in May of 2002, Joe stated three things to Terry:

1. I will stay involved only as long as you want me here;
2. You and I may disagree behind closed doors but once those doors are opened, I will support you 100 percent; and
3. If I do something you do not like, do not let it ride. Tell me.

Terry has now been at Edens for three years. During this time, he has doubled the size of the company from $1.25 billion of assets to $2.5 billion. And Joe has remained as chairman of the board. Terry's original 5-year contract expires in early 2007.

Joe Edens' successor process is a wonderful learning experience for every family business. Joe's process was masterful. Think about what we have learned:

- Joe thought long and hard about the qualifications, skills, and values he wanted in a successor;
- Joe, over a three-year time period, "tested out" people that he knew;
- Joe dealt realistically with his children's competencies and level of maturity;
- Joe involved his family and board in the process;
- Joe dealt directly with the one internal candidate;
- Joe thought through the transition process and became heavily invested in its success; and
- Once Joe made the decision, while he may have had many mixed emotions internally, he was unwavering externally.

I asked Joe how could he have so effectively given up the reins. He said, "I loved my company and what it stood for and I mean it. I had to do what is in the best interests of the company out of love and caring. I wanted the company to live successfully after me. I had gotten to the point in my life that if I really cared for the company, I needed to do something for it. You see, it was not about me—it was about my family, my employees, and yes, my legacy."

We have focused on what Joe did to make the transition successful. It is just as important to focus on what Terry did to make it successful from Joe's viewpoint.

According to Joe, "Terry did not come in like Attila the Hun and make tidal waves immediately. To the contrary, Terry came in and evaluated the people, the processes, and the quality of work product to assess who would be on his team."

After one year, Terry started making changes. He came to Joe and asked for input and advice, since all of the changes involved people Joe had hired. Joe said, "Put your team in place. It is your ship to captain."
The Edens story is really unique for three reasons:

1. It worked;
2. It is rare for a family business builder to be so open about his thoughts and processes; and
3. It is highly unusual to have the retiring CEO and the successor outsider comfortable enough to share with all of us the details and issues they dealt with.

We have heard Joe's side of the story; how about Terry's? As an outsider, what were Terry's concerns? Terry had three main concerns:

1. How the relationship with the internal candidate would evolve;
2. Making it clear as to what Terry's role and Joe's role would be; and
3. Determining if Joe really would let go.

Terry's concerns were that he knew how hard it was for entrepreneurs to "let go of their baby" and although Joe was saying the right words— would he act accordingly.
Terry had never, like most people, been in the position of negotiating with an entrepreneur to be his or her successor, and he had not been an outsider brought in to lead a company. He had CEO experience but was trained and promoted from within by his mentor at Andersen.
From Terry's perspective, what did Joe do to make this work?

- Joe gave up the CEO symbols to Terry willingly and against Terry's wishes, Joe moved offices;
- Joe became a full-time public relations person for Terry both internally in the company and externally in the community;
- The whole Edens family went out of their way to make Terry and his family welcome to Columbia and part of the Columbia community and were tireless advocates;
- Joe willingly spent three hours a day with Terry behind closed doors teaching him about the company and the people, and
- Joe never ever disagreed or voiced any hesitation in public about Terry's actions or changes.

What was in Terry's mind when he went into Edens & Avant? What did he have to do to make the succession work? Terry was very cognizant and mindful that he was not the founder of the company and that Edens and Avant would never be his company. Joe's name was on the door and the Founder had to be respected, honored, and had to be perceived as still playing a key role as Founder. Terry knew that Joe, like most successful business builders, was control-oriented. So Terry worked hard on a daily basis to keep Joe informed so there would be no surprises.

Terry, being a Southerner, understood that the employees wanted the history, tradition, and values of the company to be respected. He knew employees would look to see if there was discord between him and Joe.

Terry made symbolic changes showing this respect. Joe never had pictures of his father's grocery business nor of Edens' first shopping centers displayed. Terry had those pictures hung in his office.

"The pictures are our linkage on a daily basis to our heritage and illustrate our duties as stewards."

Terry intentionally took his time before making any big changes. Edens & Avant was not broken. Terry had time and it was 12 months before he made a change and one and a half years before he started changing senior management and putting in a new technology system and a performance-based compensation and measurement system. When Terry arrived, he inherited 24 senior officers. As of February 2005, 14 of those 24 are still with the company. Terry wanted to keep the Edens culture of integrity, do what you say, teamwork and family, and impose upon it a higher level of performance expectations.

In looking back on his first three years at the company, what would Terry, with the benefit of hindsight do differently as the successor? Terry stated:

> First, I would have done more planning upfront with Joe on a 5–12 month agreed-upon action plan—prioritizing what I needed to do. Second, I would have made more changes faster. I delayed making decisions about people and processes too long in deference to how things had been done. In hindsight, Joe understood the kind of changes I needed to make more than I thought he did. And I underestimated the pressures and the focus that employees put on the CEO. Employees want you to act, speak, and dress like a CEO. There is a way that employees want the CEO to be. I did not understand the image part of the role and learned quickly that everything I do, say, etc. is watched in the community. I became a CEO at age 40. I was concerned was I experienced enough. Looking back on it, I was slow in putting my imprint on the Company and although I joined in May of 2002, I really did not have a company-wide meeting until September of 2003.

As Terry and Joe approach their third anniversary in May of 2005, Joe still comes into the office every day and is there for Terry. Joe recently re-

minded Terry that he "would move out whenever Terry wants" and to prepare for that eventuality someday, Joe finished in December 2004 building
his new home office, which is a high tech museum quality showpiece of
Joe's hobbies and family.

Terry has performed well and is becoming an industry leader. The technology and culture transitions are still underway and the company is im-
proving its capital structure and continues to refine its strategy. The
company has decentralized its operations, sold about 25 percent of its port-
folio and increased its development activities.

Joe and the Board want to extend Terry's contract. If the company continues to operate successfully and if the board is able to successfully negotiate a new contract with Terry as his current contract ends in spring of
2007, then maybe Joe Edens will have been able to do what neither his
grandfather nor father were able to do—successfully steward and preserve
the values, legacy, and financial fortune of a successful business for others
to enjoy.

Yes, the true legacy of any family business is determined by its leader's
ability to successfully and proactively manage the passage onward to others. And as Joe stated, "with love and caring turn it over to a new captain
of the ship."

There is much to be learned from this wonderful man, Joe Edens, and
his story.

Chapter 15

Sale of the Business

Many times family businesses find themselves in the situation where the best means of maintaining family wealth is to consider selling the business. This can occur when there is no family successor; or when industry or business changes dictate that an exit now is the best way to preserve family wealth. Those industry or business changes can include industry consolidation, the entrance of a well-capitalized competitor, the ending of a product cycle, the high risk of the loss of a key customer, off-shoring of manufacturing, increased low-cost competition, and the inability of the company to grow.

The business world is volatile and hyper-competitive. The life cycle of businesses is becoming shorter and the pressures for industry consolidation are strong. Manufacturing and technology-based businesses are especially vulnerable. Service businesses, franchise, and local real estate development businesses are less volatile, less globally influenced, and not as subject to low-cost foreign competition.

If a family has not prepared a successor, either from within the family or from the business, the family may be forced to sell the business. With all due respect, if the business is viable, strong, and sustainable, such a result is inexcusable—a breach of duty to the family. It is the duty of the CEO, the board, and senior family members to prepare for and manage this risk.

Likewise, if the family business has reached its limits of growth and the business cannot support the large family, then the family can either sell the business or start another business, making the family business a little conglomerate.

If the family's goal was to build a sustainable multi-generational business, a sale should represent a major event caused by something unexpected—assuming good management and proper planning.

In the case of this unexpected event, the decision to consider selling the business can be painful for families because it can mean that no one in the family is qualified to or wants to carry on the legacy of the business. On the other hand, sometimes these decisions are motivated by realistic assessment of industry factors, the business's competitive position, or the realization that the business has peaked and it is in the best interests of the family to harvest the hard work through a sale. Absent a monopoly position or an exclusive distribution relationship (like an Anheuser Busch distributor), the realities of a global, competitive business world are competition and change.

So, if you make the decision to sell, what are your goals or obligations to the family and to your employees? For the family, the number one goal should be value maximization. Value maximization involves not only receiving the highest after-tax price, but also receiving that price in a financially liquid form.

What is a financially liquid form? Cash or non-restricted easily tradable stock in a mid-cap or large-cap public company. Many times, family businesses can be sold easily on an installment sale basis where the buyer makes a cash down payment and gives the seller a note to be paid over 5–10 years. The seller is financing the purchase and in most such cases, the seller's receipt of those deferred monies is dependent upon the performance of the business. In other words, if you sell and finance the buyer's purchase you are incurring all the risks of operating the business with no daily input and no control. And why run the risk of operations if you are selling for good business reasons?

Many of my clients ask me what they should do when they are offered two prices for the business—one in cash which is the lower price—the second on a deferred payment note. In these cases, first do not lose sight of the reasons that motivated the sale. Secondly, have your CFO or accountant do a discounted cash flow (DCF) computation using a risk discount rate of 10–20 percent, depending on your facts. Then compare the net present value (NPV) of the deferred sale versus the 100 percent cash sale.

In 30 years, I have learned two hard lessons:

- CASH is King; and
- STUFF happens.

I advise my clients to seek cash or easily tradable, highly liquid, nonvolatile public company stock. However, sometimes installment sale is your only alternative. In those cases, seek legal advice and get rights of inspection of the financials and get rights to take over the business upon the first signs of trouble. You need to legally manage the risk of default and diminution of your collateral, including limitations on the buyer's ability to withdraw directly or indirectly, property or cash from the business in any manner (other than an agreed-upon reasonable salary) and limitations on the sale of assets directly or indirectly, unless 100 percent of the proceeds are used to pay you—the seller. It is critical that you have wise, experienced

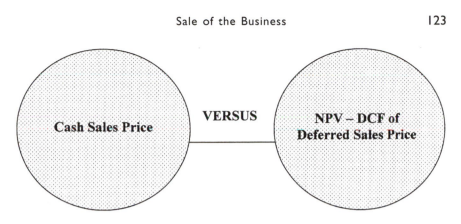

Figure 15.1. Sales Price Comparison

legal and tax advice when considering a sale of the business, especially if you are going to finance the buyer.

If you have a cash buyer for the business who is willing to pay $10 million, with limited recourse against you for warranties and representations, and another buyer willing to pay, for example, $12 million over five to seven years with 20 percent down payment, you should strongly consider taking the cash offer and have 100 percent of the control over your financial future.

Selling a business involves two distinct processes:

1. Getting the business ready to sell—"scrubbing the patient"; and

2. Creating a competitive, focused, intense auction process and managing that process.

In most cases families need outside help to do both step 1—"Scrubbing the Patient" and step 2—Managing the Process. Do not go to market without "scrubbing the patient." Outside independent professional financial advisors can objectively and realistically evaluate the strengths and weaknesses of the business and determine how to position or package the business for sale. Likewise, they are more skilled in negotiating with buyers and can play the "heavy" or "tough cop" role better than sellers who are emotionally involved in what they have built.

One key to an effective sales process is choosing the right advisor—someone whom you can trust and who has a provable and referenceable track record of loyalty to his or her clients and a track record of results. Choose someone with experience, wisdom, integrity, and judgment and who personally will spend his or her time on your sale and not delegate most of the work to younger, inexperienced assistants.

Choose someone who has the time available to be intimately involved in all negotiations and who will commit to personal involvement during the 6–12 month process. Lastly, choose someone who has no conflicts of interest or financial relationships with any potential buyers. Make sure your advisor has no financial interest, directly or indirectly (other than your fee), in choosing a buyer. Buyers can try to influence the outcome by offering your advisor future work. When hiring advisors, watch out for senior advisors who are very interested in you until you hire them, then the junior people do the work. This is called "bait and switch" in the investment banking industry. Name the person with whom you want to work in your retention agreement. Along with a financial advisor, you will need sophisticated experienced legal expertise—a lawyer who has represented many sellers and who is a "deal doer" not a "deal killer."

Good advisors keep their egos out of the deal and are willing to abide by the client's wishes and ultimate business judgments. Good advisors are costly but in my experience it is money well spent.

You will most likely sell your business only once and you will most likely only sell one business in your career, so you do not want advisors obtaining their experience through your deal—"OJT" (on-the-job-training). Pay the money and get the best advisor you can afford. Most financial advisors will work for a retainer plus a contingent success fee, plus reimbursable expenses.

Preparing to sell a business is a time-consuming process but one that saves an immense amount of time and frustration when a potential buyer conducts due diligence. During this "scrubbing the patient" phase, the goal is to find and correct any and all deficiencies that a buyer would find upon due diligence and to ensure legal compliance in the areas of corporate, tax, human resources, pension, and employment laws. Usually this includes the preparation of audited or reviewed financial statements and an intellectual property audit and opinion, if applicable. Reviewing all the corporate books, contracts, minutes, lawsuits, and grievances can take a couple of weeks but by solving and resolving issues before going to market, you are more likely not to have major due diligence issues and price renegotiations at the end of the due diligence process.

In addition, some family businesses are quite liberal on the expense side of the ledger with the results being lower income or earnings from the business. Most family businesses are not managed or operated as if they were a public company. Prior to going to market, you need to reformat or restate the operating results of the family business as if it were a non-family business. By that I mean that compensation to family members needs to be normalized to market rates and certain operating expenses (with full reconciliation and disclosure to buyer) be reclassified as if a public company owned the business. The goal is to sell normalized cash flow—sell what the business can produce for the buyer, regardless of how you withdrew the money.

Common problems arising during this preparation phase are: inadequate legal documentation of corporate records; inadequate compliance and documentation with respect to age, race, and gender discrimination laws; inadequate environmental or OSHA documentation; inadequate protection of intangible assets; failure to get full releases from claim, lawsuits, or aggrieved employees; liberal credit policies; inadequate bad debt reserves; above-market leases of assets (real estate) owned by the family; above-market family compensation; expensive company cars; liberal family expense reimbursement; liberal entertainment and travel expenses; liberal family education reimbursements; and environmental issues.

While the business is being scrubbed, you and your advisors need to simultaneously determine the range of values for your business and who the likely buyers are. Valuation determinations are dependent upon your industry, the strength and weaknesses of your business, the value of its future likely cash flows, the intangible value of your organization, brand and customer lists, and the specific strategic value to a specific buyer. Buyers buy for two general reasons: greed and fear.

Greed is obvious. Everyone wants to make money from their investment. Fear is not so obvious. I have seen many buyers overpay because of fear—fear that a competitor would be the buyer and as a result, the competitor would be a stronger, more viable competitor.

Valuation is part art and part science and again the general metrics are multiples of cash flow or EBITDA (earnings before interest, taxes, depreciation, and amortization) and are dependent in large part on your industry. As part of the science of valuation, you should do five-year projections of the likely business results for your company and utilize these projections as a base for discussion purposes. The future may impact a buyer's view of the past. By that I mean, a realistically optimistic future may generate a higher multiplier on your current income.

In addition to valuation work, you and your advisors need to create a list of potential buyers. There are two broad, generic types of buyers—financial buyers and strategic buyers. Financial buyers are private equity funds or wealthy individuals whose business is investing in different businesses for financial returns. These buyers usually look for both good management and opportunity. Sometimes they will buy without good management in place if the acquired business is to be consolidated or merged with a similar business that the buyer already owns. Or when they have a stable of successful managers to place in the business.

Financial buyers make money by buying at one multiple and after 3–7 years selling more EBIDA at a higher multiple. Financial buyers can be very competitive buyers if they know the industry and if they have investment capital that they need to invest as soon as possible. Historically, financial buyers generally paid lower prices than strategic buyers. But as the amount of investment capital has grown, now a motivated cash-rich financial buyer can compete price-wise with any strategic buyer.

The second generic type of buyer is a strategic buyer—generally a company that is a competitor of yours or is a company in your industry wanting to expand geographically, or wanting your customer relationships, or wanting to prevent someone else from acquiring the same. Generally speaking, strategic buyers have lower rates of return requirements than financial buyers and usually can outbid financial buyers.

Thus, when making up your buyer list, it should include both financial buyers and strategic buyers, if possible. Financial buyers can be found in reference books or on-line and through industry trade news. Financial buyers usually can be qualified by the geography in which they will invest, the size of deals they will do, and the industries in which they concentrate. I cannot stress enough industry research through trade associations and newsletters. Generally speaking, it is not hard to learn what players are active real buyers for your type of business.

If your business is too small for a financial buyer or strategic buyer, then you need to look for an individual buyer in your geography or through advertising your sale a buyer wanting to either move to or invest in your geographic area. Again, this is a process of targeting the right potential buyers. Here again, experienced advisors should have worked with many such buyers.

So once you have "scrubbed the patient," done your valuation work, and prepared your potential buyer list, you should prioritize your goals and objectives of a sale—financially personally, and for your employees. Are you willing to stay on as a 2–3 year transition CEO? Are you willing to sell and leave immediately? Are you concerned whether your employees get laid off as a result of the sale? What steps have you taken to protect and ensure that key employees who represent the company's future income potential (which affects your sales price) are or will be taken care of? Are they under employment contracts with non-competes? Do you wish to retain ownership of the real estate?

So let the games begin. Your advisor should have prepared a short sales summary that is utilized to generate interested buyers. This sale document has only one purpose—to identify interested parties and to motivate them to visit with you as soon as possible. This sales summary is not a due diligence document; it should be a short, concise, compelling story of why your company is a valuable opportunity for the right purchaser.

The key to a sales process is for your advisor to: (1) create a sense of urgency; (2) get buyers to the table as soon as possible; (3) create a competition among the interested buyers; (4) find out as soon as possible the major issues of each buyer; (5) determine the buyers' motivations, obstacles to closing, or hurdles to overcome, and (6) determine what person has the authority to commit and what is and how much time their respective buying process will take. During the buying process, you need to expose and negotiate all key issues before choosing a buyer.

Table 15.1
The Timeline

January 1–February 15	"Scrub the patient" Prepare sales document Identify potential buyers
February 15–February 28	Invite buyers to participate
March	Meetings with buyers
April	Offers due Negotiations Rebidding Narrowing the field Final bids
April 30	Sign letter of intent
May	Due diligence and legal documentation
June 15	Closing legal documents agreed to
June 30	Closing

If done well, a sales process can be accomplished start to finish in 6 months. If done poorly, you could be looking at 12 months or more. The reason time is so important is that businesses do not stand still—stuff changes, stuff happens—and usually the stuff lowers the value of a business rather than raising the value.

A competition amongst bidders is critical. Having more than one bidder and having those bidders bid against each other is critical because only through that process can you determine what market value is and a bidding process keeps the bidders "honest." While you are going through this bidding process, it is as important that you use the process to discuss and negotiate critical deal points. I have never had a buyer make his only or his best bid in his first bid.

I advise clients to negotiate all the key points of a deal before signing a letter of intent that will terminate discussions with all other bidders. Once you sign the letter of intent, you lose much of your negotiating leverage. That is, your negotiating position changes (lessens). Once you sign a letter of intent, the other bidders go on to other businesses and they know they were not your first choice. And if you were to return, they know you had a problem and some use this to their advantage in negotiating a lower price.

A couple of points to stress about the sales process—in negotiating the letter of intent or the term sheet, you want to talk with all bidders about every possible money issue. Those issues include:

- Sales price;
- Payment terms;
- Restrictions on currency received, if any;
- Holdbacks or earn-outs, if any;
- Liability for breaches of warranties and representations—both time limits, scope, and monetary limits;
- Payment of deal expenses;
- Contingencies to closing and to payment;
- If applicable, employment terms, compensation, benefits, and options;
- Covenants not to compete; and
- Any potential liability of the seller after the deal closes, if any.

Many buyers try to structure a deal so as to include an earn-out. Your receipt of some of your sales price would be subject to the business generating the projected earnings. I do not like earn-outs. My experience with them is that they are likely to end up in dispute or litigation. Once you sell your business, in most cases, you lose control. You cannot control the timing of revenue generation, the timing of expenses, the magnitude of corporate overhead allocations, and the business's performance. Like an installment sale, an earn-out places your financial return in someone else's hands.

One very important point for you personally to fully think through is that once you sell your business, it is not your business. And if you agree to stay on with the buyer, you will be an employee. You will have a boss and in most cases, this transition for a family business owner is very, very difficult. You no longer can spend what you want; work when you want; and do it your way. Most of my clients have not fared well transitioning to an employee and most leave the buyer within two years.

Once you reach the letter of intent stage, you cannot lessen the intensity and focus. Unless managed, buyers due diligence can take months and drag on and on. It is important to agree on a due diligence time frame prior to signing the letter of intent and to adhere to it. Because of all the "scrubbing" work you did before going to market, your advisors should have all the documents ready for the buyer's team. Absent special circumstances, due diligence should be completed in 45 days.

The business world is full of stories about buyers who bid high, win auction processes and then after due diligence, retrade or renegotiate the price downward, sometimes substantially. How do you protect against that? Although there is no perfect way, the best way is to talk with other people who sold to your buyer before you sign the letter of intent. Ask them directly whether the buyer attempted to retrade. In other words, before signing a letter of intent, do your best to do your due diligence on your buyer, its track record in closing and whether they were honest people.

Due diligence document review should be handled away from the business and buyer visits to the business should be managed, limited, and always escorted to prevent disruptions and employee misunderstandings. The first reaction—which is normal—of employees is "Will I lose my job, my position?" Also, you should understand that just because you signed a letter of intent that does *not* mean your business is sold. Your deal may or may not actually close depending on the results of due diligence, the motivations of the buyer, and outside macro economics, stock market, industry, or buyer factors.

As I tell clients, until the wire transfer hits, you own the business and do not pre-spend sales money before you receive it. I had one client who immediately upon signing a letter of intent made a large personal purchase. Unfortunately, his deal did not close.

What kills deals? Surprises, lies, trying to retrade the deal, and advisors who are trying to out-advise the other side or who are trying too hard to improve your business deal. Hire good advisors who are deal closers and who can advise you of the risks, quantify those risks, and allow you to make your own best business judgments.

While you are spending all of this time trying to sell the business, remember do not forget the business. Revenue declines, lost customers, and other problems can lower your price right up to closing. And as importantly, your sale may not close so take care of your "golden goose."

Chapter 16

Going Public or Recapitalizing Your Family Business

Family businesses, like most businesses, face critical inflection points in their history when certain decisions change or chart the course of the business for years to come. Critical decisions can be proactive or reactive. Proactive decisions can be strategic—buying a source of revenue or merging with a competitor or consolidator or raising capital to buy out unhappy family shareholders.

Reactive decisions are decisions forced by others. For example, shareholders want to be bought out or shareholders want liquidity; or shareholders want to maximize their stock value in the public markets. It could also be that your industry is consolidating, or your market is shrinking and you need capital or public company stock as currency for making acquisitions or diversification investments.

It should be no surprise to you that I strongly support proactive management—staying ahead of the problems, if possible. Being aware of potential problems and developing different scenarios to deal with them. And when appropriate, taking steps to solve those problems before they become big problems. Big problems can force you to sell your company or sell part of your company to the public or to a private equity partner.

This chapter will discuss two sources of equity capital—the public markets (initial public offering [IPO]) and private equity funds. I have advised clients on the raising of approximately $5 billion in the public and private equity markets during my career. Raising capital either in the public or the private markets involves a major personal, philosophical, and probably even a cultural change for a family business.

Most families focus intensely on the money to be received from an IPO or a private equity recapitalization. Unfortunately, few focus on the dramatic operating and cultural changes the family business will undergo when it no longer is a family business.

If you go public or if you bring in an outside private equity partner, you will no longer be a family business.

What does that mean? It means that family considerations in making business decisions are over. The only concern now is the creation of shareholder value for you and your new shareholders. You will have to conduct your business and make decisions on an arm's-length basis like a public company and you cannot do things solely in the best interests of the family.

In other words, if you decide to go public or to do a private equity recapitalization, the game is changed; it is no longer solely your business. Your board of directors will most likely change. Your accountants and lawyers will most likely change. You will have to change how family members interact with the business. The business is no longer the "family piggy bank." Its assets are no longer yours. Any and all transactions or expenditures for, by, or with the family will be curtailed or at least heavily scrutinized and held to market standards. That means salaries, perks, benefits, country club dues, cars, travel and entertainment, and expense reimbursements will be on a market rate arm's-length basis. What I am saying is do not underestimate the magnitude, severity, and degree of this change. Seek the advice of families who have taken these steps before you decide. Learn from their experiences.

No matter what the investment bankers tell you, the change is not minimal; it is severe. For example, in my experience, many family business leaders do not have the skills or personality to be a public company CEO. Or in the case of a private equity recapitalization, many family business leaders do not have the willingness, demeanor, or interest to operate in a partnership manner with the new equity partner. Family CEOs are used to doing what they want, when they want, and how they want. No longer will it solely be your family business. You will have either public shareholders or an equity partner with whom you must consult with often about any and all major business decisions and in most cases, such partners must consent for you to do what you want to do.

In the case of a private equity recapitalization, most family leaders do not think ahead prospectively about how they will meet the needs of that partner to realize its financial returns in five years. How does the new equity partner get bought out—by whom and when? Such investors will pressure you to realize their returns when they need them, not when it is necessarily in the best interests of the business. Investors may need returns because they are raising new funds and need to show a good track record. Investors may need to exit because they want to invest their money elsewhere. Investors may not be patient with long-term investments or family members' work habits or company expenditures on entertainment or health insurance coverage for family members. When investors want their money back, you will have to either borrow a large amount of debt; find another investor—replace one problem with a prospective different problem; or sell the company. None of those alternatives may be easy or desirable. Many people fail to think ahead and see that solving one problem now creates another problem in the future by bringing on an equity partner. Although I have heard of 10-year investments by private equity investors, I have never experienced that type of long-term view. My experience is that while most investors say they have a long-term view, within 3 to 5 years of making the investment, they want their financial returns.

GOING PUBLIC

Many business builders and families fantasize about going public as the way to institutionalize their company. There are valid reasons to go public. As an example, Sam Walton took Wal-Mart public to repay substantial bank debt incurred in store expansions and to raise capital for more store openings. I advised a family business owned by four brothers and sisters to go public as a means to create a reliable dividend flow for the three siblings not working in the business and to access capital for growth. Generally speaking, valid reasons are to de-leverage—change debt to equity and to have access to lower cost growth capital or acquisition currency in the form of public company stock.

Most people I have worked with want to go public to get rich quickly. That usually does not happen. First, in most IPOs, the founding family is limited in the amount of cash they can receive in the IPO and after the IPO, there are usually underwriter restrictions on sale by control shareholders as well as practical market liquidity and market perception restrictions. In most cases, you will have to liquefy your stock slowly and sell in dribbles over years and your ability to do that will depend on the liquidity in the stock and how well you perform meeting quarterly earnings expectations.

Before going public, understand when and under what circumstances you can sell your stock and understand the prior experience of previous IPOs—how many have seen their stock price fall after the IPO? And understand what will happen to your public market value if you do not perform or if you have to restate earnings or if you are late reporting. The public markets can be fickle and non-forgiving. In such cases, your newfound wealth through a public market valuation can evaporate.

Some of my clients have thought that the public markets were preferable to all the family issues. What they found out was that the family issues remained and in addition, they had new constituencies who were more demanding and who also had to be managed—stock analysts, large institutional shareholders, and retail investors.

BEING A PUBLIC COMPANY CEO

Let me return to the issue of whether the family business CEO has the skills and personality to be a public company CEO. To be an effective public company CEO, you have to have the will and ability not only to manage the business but to collaborate with an independent board and to communicate frequently with stock analysts and institutional shareholders.

In many cases, such stock analysts or the representatives of the institutional shareholders can be financial engineering MBAs who are very bright and very young but have little hands-on business experience. And you have to listen to their views and treat them with respect.

Understand also that you were able to go public because you convinced everyone that you would grow. And you had better grow quickly and keep on growing every quarter. Young public companies must meet quarterly earnings expectations and must grow every quarter to maintain their stock price and following. This new pressure is completely foreign to a family business CEO who has never had the intense short-term focus. I have had several public company CEOs say that they did not believe me before going public but that the public markets quarterly earnings growth pressure is very difficult to adjust to.

GOING PUBLIC—UNDERWRITING

Let us assume you are going public for the right reasons and you have a realistic understanding of what it means to operate as a public company and that you have the skills, competencies, personality and demeanor to be a public company CEO. So far, so good. Now you need to find an underwriter.

Underwriters are regulated broker-dealers who assist you in raising the money through their sales force and the sales force of others. Underwriters are investment bankers and are organized into different groups of people by function—deal originators, deal evaluators, and deal sellers.

Deal originators are the sales force and they are called investment bankers. Their job is to bring in business and to close a percentage of that business. Some investment bankers work on a volume basis; they bring in ten deals and hope to close three or four. Other investment bankers try to close a higher percentage and take on fewer clients. Closing percentage is key. Most people assume their deal is closed when they hire an investment banker. Not necessarily so.

The investment banker's job is to convince you to hire his or her firm and not a competitor. They are first and foremost a sales function. In determining which investment banker to hire, first you should check out their track record and references. Second, you need to understand the commonly used "bait and switch" ploy where you think you are hiring a very senior investment banker and then after your retention agreement is signed, you are passed off to a less experienced, younger person who on a daily basis handles your deal.

The second important person in the investment banking world is the quality control reviewer or the research analyst. Historically, the research analyst was the independent quality control function in the investment bank. In the 1980s and 1990s, this function was co-opted into an investment banking function but now in some firms after the Internet, technology, and telecom bubbles, the research function is being revitalized as an independent quality control function. This is the person who has a large say in whether you will go public and at what price. No problem except that most people choose their underwriter based on the investment banker's sales pitch and never meet the research analyst until after they have picked the underwriter. Wrong. You should meet the research analyst and do a road show presentation for him or her and understand their opinions about you, your company, its viability as a public company and your potential stock pricing before you choose an underwriter.

The third functional area of an investment bank are the people that will actually make the sales calls to mutual funds and individual investors to sell your stock—the institutional and retail sales force—and the syndicate manager who will bring in other selling firms. Most people falsely think that if my investment banker likes my deal, it will sell. You should, before choosing an underwriter, meet the sales executives and get their direct feedback on whether they think you are a good public company candidate. To go public successfully, in most cases you need the buy-in and enthusiasm of three people—the investment banker, the quality control person, and the sales force executive. Mitigate your risks and manage your process so you know that you have all three approvals prior to choosing an underwriter.

VALUATION OF YOUR COMPANY

Whether you are contemplating an IPO or private equity recapitalization, valuation of your business will be critical to the accomplishment of your objectives. In the public markets, the valuation will be ultimately set by the amount of interest in your stock. In the underwriter selection process, you should request and receive the investment bank's opinion of your valuation—which will likely be a range of values. Public market valuations can be impacted by macro-economic events, political events, industry events, competitor actions, and the supply of IPO products in the market or being brought to market at the same time by your underwriter. Understand all of these factors and talk about them with the potential investment banks.

The stock market is governed as much by perception and supply and demand as by valuation fundamentals. But the important point is that as you go through the underwriter selection process, have each firm give you a written valuation report that will show you (as a group) consensus methodology. Again, in the IPO process, your ultimate valuation will be set at the closing by the market and the underwriter.

In the private equity process, your valuation is determined by each private equity firm seeking or bidding to be your new partner. And the only way to increase your probability of getting a fair valuation is to have more than one firm bidding. Only a competitive bidding process between or among competing private equity firms will produce a market value. You may choose a lower value bidder for strategic or personality fit, but at least you will have a better idea of value.

You should have seen a commonality to the valuation issue in both the IPO and the private equity process. I am a big believer in managed competitions, having several underwriters or buyers or private equity players bid in a competitive, intense, short process for your company. A competitive bidding process is the only way to assure family shareholders that you have looked at the market diligently.

OTHER FACTORS

In deciding whether to go public or sell part of your family business to a private equity firm, of course you need to "scrub" your company and normalize it as if it were a public company before starting the talking process. This could take 1–2 months, depending on the degree of legal and accounting compliance and clean-up you need to do.

You need also to obtain experienced legal and accounting advisors with IPO or private equity experience. You do not want advisors learning on your case. And you need to understand the out-of-pocket costs needed to enter the game. Generally, the expense of going public will cost you 10 percent of the monies raised and raising private equity generally could cost you up to 7 percent of the monies raised if you use a financial advisor. All costs depend on the size of your deal and the complexity of the deal.

How much time will it take to do a deal? Usually 6–12 months unless you have major issues. And the time required of you as the CEO will be substantial. Therefore, you need to have a plan for managing the business while you spend 50–75 percent of your time on fund raising. Too many people overlook this point and the business performs poorly while you are in the money raising process. Guess what? If that occurs, your valuation may decline or your investor or investment banker may withdraw.

In the last two chapters, we have talked about liquidity events, exit events, and ways to access growth capital. Going public, or bringing in a private equity partner, or selling the business are major once-in-a-business-lifetime events. Each has its pros and cons. Each have risks, ramifications, and process idiosyncrasies. I cannot express enough to you that:

1. You need experienced, competent (and usually that means relatively costly) advisors with verifiable track records and references;

2. You need a managed, competitive process that you begin after you and your advisors have prepared ("scrubbed") your company for inspection;

3. You need multiple bidders rebidding in an auction-like process to really determine market value;

4. You need someone to manage the business during the process;

5. You need to understand that every deal goes through emotional highs and emotional lows and that deals seem to die a couple of times during any process—but they do come back to life. Also remember that in any case, a deal is never done until the wire transfer hits and whatever you do, do not spend expected or hoped-for deal money prior to its actual receipt;

6. These types of major transactions will change your family business and your job as CEO. Your independence, autonomy, and control will be lost. You will become an employee;

7. Most family business CEOs have a hard time becoming an employee; and

8. Take your time—speak to families who have gone through the process—understand and explain fully to all family shareholders the pros and cons of each alternative, the risks of the venture, and what it means for the family and for them.

Chapter 17

Family Business Operating Rules

RULE 1

Your chance of building a sustainable, successful business increases if you adopt one performance and review standard for all employees based on merit and arm's-length business dealings. There should not be two performance, promotion, or HR policies—one for family and one for non-family employees.

RULE 2

Family members beginning in the business should not report to or be evaluated by their parents, aunts, or uncles. They should be taught, mentored, and critiqued by trusted senior employees.

RULE 3

From a risk management viewpoint, there should be a limit on the number of family members employed from each generation or branch of the family to limit rivalries. Remember—if you have five children working in the business, there will only be one CEO spot; you will have four disappointed children.

RULE 4

Family members should be required to work a minimum number of years elsewhere and receive outstanding performance reviews before coming to work in the family business. This will allow them to earn the respect of other employees and to build their own self-esteem and confidence because they did "make it" in the real world.

RULE 5

HIRE and
REWARD and
PROMOTE and
DEMOTE
family employees based on need and merit.

RULE 6

Never, never condone family employee arrogance, hubris, or flaunting of one's family position over other employees or customers.

RULE 7

Family members will only be hired to fill need-specific positions and will be paid at market rates.

RULE 8

The compensation levels of all family members and the market rate justification should be disclosed to all family shareholders.

RULE 9

All family shareholders have legal rights. Respect them.

RULE 10

Family members should earn their way and earn the respect of other employees.

RULE 11

Corporate benefits or perks should be administered fairly, consistently, and in such a manner as does not hurt the business culture.

RULE 12

The issue of dividends, in most cases, is an issue of educating shareholders about the business's financial needs and it should be discussed at each Annual Family Meeting.

RULE 13

In most cases, you should keep the family business CFO or controller focused on their business job and not on taking care of family personal matters.

RULE 14

Minority shareholders have legal rights and majority shareholders owe them fiduciary duties.

RULE 15

Adopt rules relating to employment, stock ownership, inheritance, and divorce settlements before you have problems. Keep it simple.

RULE 16

Divorce should end an in-law's involvement in any way with the family business and should be so stated prior to marriage and prior to employment.

RULE 17

The family business should buy all its products and services on an arm's-length market rate basis. Buying from family members is okay if fully disclosed to all shareholders and if the rule of market rate is consistently and fairly applied.

RULE 18

Retirement planning is an integral part of succession planning for the first generation and should be a five-year implementation process—a long enough time to test a potential successor and to give the retiree time and opportunity to find new challenges.

RULE 19

Generational succession should cover employment, stock ownership, and retirement benefits, if any; and

RULE 20

Generational succession should plan for passing voting control to successor generations.

RULE 21

Every family business issue should be viewed from two viewpoints:

1. What is best for the business?

and

2. What is best for the family?

RULE 22

You want a knowledgeable, financially literate family shareholder group. To this end you should communicate financial results fully and often and educate shareholders about the business.

RULE 23

Board structure becomes more and more important as the number of shareholders and generations increase and as the geographical dispersion of shareholders increase.

RULE 24

Structure the board to accomplish your objectives of family involvement, input, and education.

RULE 25

Use charitable contributions to foster family involvement in the business and favor the charities of non-employed family members.

RULE 26

Do not have brothers or sisters reporting to siblings or cousins.

RULE 27

Do not have siblings or cousins reporting to parents.

RULE 28

Although I have *heard* of it working in a few cases, I have never personally *seen* co-anything work. By that, I mean co-CEOs or co-chairman positions.

RULE 29

Remember the Sandbox Theory:

Everyone needs and wants their own sandbox to play in.

RULE 30

Rivalries are normal and they must be managed proactively and pre-emptively. The *Sandbox Theory* is the best way I have seen rivalries managed. Rivalries can be managed by structuring distinct and separate areas of responsibilities for each family member—separate by business function or by product or service or by geographical location.

RULE 31

Succession planning is a must for every family business regardless of the age of the family leader. Who will run the business in the case of an unexpected death or disability?

RULE 32

Retirement succession should be planned over a 5–10 year period so that (a) the retiree can create new opportunities and meaningful challenges to move onto; and (b) the successor can learn and earn the trust and respect of the employees, the customers, and the family.

RULE 33

If there is no family successor, then the ideal successor should know the industry, know the business, and have already earned the trust and respect of the employees and the family either by working in the business or working for the family in some capacity.

RULE 34

Succession planning is one of the highest duties and responsibilities of the CEO to the family, to the employees, and to the customers—a responsibility to plan ahead so that the dream of the business can be realized and a true legacy established.

RULE 35

Succession planning is never easy but it can become easier if it becomes an institutionalized annual process whereby a written succession plan is agreed upon at each Annual Family Meeting in the case of an untimely, unexpected death of the CEO.

RULE 36

Succession must be a values-based discussion and decision—not a personal decision—the values of stewardship and what is best for all involved.

RULE 37

Don't forget the Sandbox Theory. In my experience, successful successions occur when the retiring CEO has a new challenge or something meaningful (a new sandbox) to move on to.

RULE 38

The successor's skills and strengths must be the best match for the business' current and near-future needs and challenges. Match skills to needs. In addition, keep in mind the new family CEO may need to become the family leader.

RULE 39

If siblings or cousins who are not chosen as CEO choose not to be good team players, then they must leave the company.

RULE 40

Play to people's strengths. Great businesses have great management teams. Play to the strengths of non-CEO family members—give them responsibilities and challenges and opportunities to grow.

RULE 41

Family members' needs will change as they age. Plan ahead for those needs. Be proactive and preempt problems.

RULE 42

The job of a family business CEO is to Communicate and Educate Often.

RULE 43

Board structure should take into account generation, family branch, gender, age, and non-business experience.

RULE 44

Family values should be discussed, taught, and constantly talked about as the foundation for decisions.

RULE 45

Do not let the business destroy the family and do not let the family destroy the business.

RULE 46

Ask yourself continually—what is in the best interest of the business? What is in the best interest of the family? What is in the best interest of the particular family member? What is in the best interest of non-family employees?

RULE 47

You cannot communicate enough.

RULE 48

Family business leaders need to listen to family concerns—remember, people want to be heard and have their views respected and be taken into consideration.

RULE 49

Top-down, patriarchal management styles can coerce family compliance only so long.

RULE 50

Include spouses in family shareholder meetings and seek their input and involvement.

RULE 51

Stock ownership should be limited to direct descendant family members.

RULE 52

Stock transfer restrictions are a must.

RULE 53

Stock buy-back plans should be considered.

RULE 54

Meaningful dividends must be paid if you have family members not working in the business.

RULE 55

The "money-pie" is only so big—the company can only afford so much.

RULE 56

Always think about equity and fairness and consistency. Trust is the glue that links family members together.

RULE 57

Always consider equity between generations and equity between family employees and family non-employees.

RULE 58

Hold quarterly board meetings and Annual Family Meetings. Involve and educate the part of the family not working in the business.

RULE 59

Disclose detailed financials to all shareholders.

RULE 60

Family issues, concerns, or problems are normal.

RULE 61

Family issues will occur in a predictive pattern as the family ages and grows.

RULE 62

You cannot manage the family like you manage the business.

RULE 63

Different skills are needed to manage the family—emotional intelligence and maturity are key.

RULE 64

If you decide to sell the business, time your exit to maximize value.

RULE 65

Selling a business is a process to be managed. A short, intense competition (auction) should produce the highest price.

RULE 66

Family business owners generally make poor employees.

RULE 67

A sale of the business or bringing in an outside partner will change the family's relationship to the business dramatically.

RULE 68

Going public is a difficult process and transaction for a family.

RULE 69

Hire experienced, wise advisors with a track record of integrity, loyalty, and success.

RULE 70

Beware of the "bait and switch" tactic of advisors.

RULE 71

Never underestimate human nature and people's tendencies toward selfishness, greed, and self-interest.

RULE 72

Family businesses succeed when the family as a whole lives the stewardship value.

RULE 73

Most family issues involve money *and* the quest for equity, recognition, opportunity, or love.

Resources

My editor, Nick Philipson—a consummate professional—asked me to consider the best business books and articles that I would recommend to you, our readers. The following is such a list of books, articles, information portals, and some of my better writings on business subjects. These resources are organized by type and then subject matter, with the authors being listed alphabetically.

BOOKS

Building a Company Books

Bethune, Gordon, *From Worst To First* (Wiley) 1998. ISBN 0–471–24835–5.
    The story of how Gordon Bethune took Continental Airlines from last place to first place. A good management, leadership, and execution book with lessons on how to keep focused on the customer.

Dell, Michael, with Catherine Freedman, *Direct From Dell* (Harper Business) 1999. ISBN 0–88730–914–3.
    From dorm room to transforming and dominating an industry, the Michael Dell story is the story of the creation of a new logistics-supply chain model, which has made just-in-time manufacturing logistics a business necessity.

Marcus, Bernie, and Arthur Blank, with Bob Andelman, *The Home Depot* (Time Business) 1999. ISBN 0–8129–3058–4.
    The story of how two fired friends rebounded to create and build the highly successful Home Depot Company. Like many other successful entrepreneurs—Sam Walton, Ross Perot, Howard Schultz—Marcus and Blank saw an opportunity in their industry which their employer did not see. And the result was that they all did it their way.

O'Reilly, Charles II, and Jeffrey Pfeffer, *Hidden Value* (HBS Publishers) 2000. ISBN 0–87584–898–2.

Stanford University's answer to "how great companies achieve extraordinary results with ordinary people" focusing on eight companies including Southwest Airlines, the Men's Wearhouse, and the SAS Institute.

Roddick, Anita, *Body and Soul* (Crown) 1991. ISBN 0–517–88134–0.

The remarkable story of how a non-business housewife opens a shop to support herself and her children while her husband leaves England to accomplish his life's goal of riding a horse across South America. From one shop to a corporate empire, to an empire lost, and regained, to a noted leader of corporate sustainability, fair trade, and corporate ethics.

Schultz, Howard, and Dori Yang, *Pour Your Heart Into It* (Hyperion) 1997. ISBN 0–7868–6397–8.

The Starbucks story from the Projects of the Bronx to the creation of a company which continues to grow. The role of values, the ground-breaking benefits given to employees, and how Howard Schultz kept his promise not to treat his employees like his father was treated. A great read about perseverance, character, and good mentors.

Truett, S. Cathy, *Eat Mor Chiken: Inspire More People* (Chick-fil-A, Inc.) 2002. ISBN 1–929619–08–1.

The story of Truett and Jeannette Cathy's journey from one restaurant to building a restaurant empire based on family values, character, and spiritual values. All Chick-fil-A stores are closed on Sundays and the Cathy Family's success has been passed on to the second generation.

Walton, Sam, with John Huey, *Sam Walton Made In America* (Bantam Books) 1993. ISBN 0–553–56283–5.

Sam Walton's autobiography. The story of how he learned from his mother to excel and to be driven to succeed and the role of his wife and daughter in influencing Wal-Mart policies. His business model and the creation of a "family" atmosphere with his employees are crucial to understanding what Wal-Mart was under Sam Walton.

Business Strategy Books

D'Aveni, Richard, *Hypercompetition* (Free Press) 1994. ISBN 0029069386.

My friend, Professor Rich D'Aveni, of the Amos Tuck School at Dartmouth, puts forth a hypercompetition model for our fast-paced, changing, volatile, global world. The importance of this book is its emphasis that one's strategy should not be static, but rather one's strategy is an iterative, evolving, proactive response to industry changes and competitor thrusts and countermoves. A dynamic approach to business strategy.

Hargadon, Andrew, *How Breakthroughs Happen: The Surprising Truth About How Companies Innovate* (HBS Press) 2003. ISBN 1–57851–904–7.

A counter-intuitive book which gives hope to us normal people that most businesses can innovate without hiring geniuses and research types. The surprising truth of Andy's research is that most innovation occurs because people take ideas, products and services from one domain to another—they move ideas across industries.

Joyce, William, Nitin Nohria, and Bruce Roberson, *What Really Works: The 4+2 Formula For Sustained Business Success* (Harper Business) 2003. ISBN 0–06–051278–4.

What makes successful companies successful? That is the million dollar question. That is the basis of my current research project, *The 6 Secrets of Organic Growth* ©. These three professors likewise set out to crack the DNA of success and came away with their 4+2 model. They share what they have learned about strategy, execution, culture, organization plus talent, leadership, innovation, and mergers.

Mintzberg, Henry, Bruce Ahlstrand, and Joseph Lampel, *Strategy Safari: A Guided Tour Through The Wilds of Strategic Management* (Prentice Hall) 1998. ISBN 0–13–695677–7.

Professor Mintzberg is a brilliant strategist. I hired him once to teach strategy to a global group of my executives and he was spell-binding. This book is a great overview of the ten competing schools of strategy with a summary of each model. These models take either an inside-out viewpoint or an outside-in viewpoint. A wonderful, thought-provoking read.

Porter, Michael E., *Competitive Strategy* (Free Press) 1980. ISBN 0–02–025360–8.

If you only ever read one book on strategy, this should be it. Professor Porter of the Harvard Business Schools gives you the methodology to analyze your industry and your competitors. His "5 Forces" are used by every company strategist I know and he clearly states that every business needs to adopt one of two strategies: A volume low-cost producer or a niche differentiator. Professor Porter taught me the overriding importance of switching costs—the difficulty in customer acquisition.

Entrepreneurship Books

Gerber, Michael E., *The E-Myth Revisited: Why Most Small Businesses Don't Work and What To Do About It* (HarperCollins) 2001. ISBN 0–88730–728–0.

This book discusses why most small businesses fail and the difficulty of an entrepreneur moving from being a doer to a manager of others.

Kuratko, Donald, and Harold Welsch, *Strategic Entrepreneurial Growth* (Harcourt) 2001. ISBN 0–03–031936–6.

A very good business school textbook on entrepreneurship, building a business, and managing a business. Includes topics of innovation, globalization, and family business succession.

McGrath, Rita, and Ian MacMillan, *The Entrepreneurial Mindset* (HBS Press) 2000. ISBN 0–87584–834–6.

The best book for learning entrepreneurial methodologies or analytical frameworks. The tools are useful no matter what the stage of your business. Discovery-driven planning, real options thinking, consumption chains, and product attribute maps are examples of useful tools. I use this book in teaching executive education to corporate leaders.

Timmons, Jeffrey A., *New Venture Creation: Entrepreneurship For The 21st Century* (Fourth Edition, McGraw-Hill) 1997. ISBN 0–256–11548–6.

The best entrepreneurship book I have found. I used this in my Emory Entrepreneurship Course. From opportunity recognition, to screening opportunities, to financing growth, to managing rapid growth, to exiting a business—this book contains great checklists and processes for every business manager.

Family Business Books

Aronoff, Craig, Joe Astrachan, and John Ward, *Developing Family Business Policies: Your Guide to the Future* (Family Enterprise Publishers) 1998. ISBN 1–891652–01–X.

A good checklist of family business policies not inconsistent with the ones I discussed. But another good source of information. Less directive than my work. The authors were also consulting partners.

Gersick, Kelin, John Davis, Marion Hampton, and Ivan Lansberg, *Generation to Generation: Life Cycles of The Family Business* (HBS Press) 1997. ISBN 0–87584–555–4.

Two academics and two consultants collaborate to put forth a model for how family businesses evolve and the different roles family members can play as family members, employees, and owners.

Lansberg, Ivan, *Succeeding Generations: Realizing the Dream of Families in Business* (HBS Press) 1999. ISBN 0–87584–742–0.

This book focuses on succession and the complex issues involved in managing a succession. A good, but long, read on marshalling a family's dream, the selection process, the governance issues, and about letting go.

Ward, John L., *Keeping The Family Business Healthy* (Business Owner Resources) 1997. ISBN 1–55542–026–5.

Fundamentally, a strategy book for managing and perpetuating a family business. A good basic primer.

Ward, John L., *Perpetrating The Family Business* (Palgrave Macmillan) 2004. ISBN 1–4039–3397–9.

This, in my opinion, is John Ward's best book—what he has learned in his 25 years teaching, researching, and consulting. This book will reinforce many of the lessons you learned in my book.

Finance, Accounting, and Measurement Books

Bruner, Robert F., *Deals From Hell: M&A Lessons That Rise Above The Ashes* (Wiley) 2005. ISBN 13–978–0–471–39595–9.

Bob Bruner is a professor at The University of Virginia Darden School of Business. I once hired Bob to teach my young associates the realities of finance. Bob is one of the leading authorities on mergers. Do they work? Under what conditions? And what are the common pitfalls? A must read for anyone thinking of merging a business or selling for stock.

Copeland, Tom, Tim Koller, and Jack Murrin, *Valuation: Measuring and Managing The Value of Companies* (Second Edition, Wiley) 1994. ISBN 0–471–36190–9.

The bible of valuation written by three McKinsey & Company professionals. This book should answer your questions on discounted cash flow projections, EBITDA versus accounting net income, the real cost of financing or capital, values-based management, and finding the value drivers of your business.

Fridson, Martin, Fernando Alvarez, and Martin S. Fridson, *Financial Statement Analysis: A Practitioner's Guide* (Third Edition, Wiley) 2002. ISBN 0–471–40915–4.

An outstanding book for those with a basic understanding of accounting. A compendium of common issues in understanding securities offerings and evaluating competitors or targets' financial statements. The ways numbers can be massaged or manipulated.

Kaplan, Robert, and David Norton, *The Balanced Scorecard: Translating Strategy Into Action* (HBS Press) 1996. ISBN 0–87584–651–3.

How do you measure results? How do you measure employee or business unit results. Many businesses today utilize some form of balanced scorecard to link measurements and strategy and to achieve strategic alignment of their different business units, departments, or functions. This book makes it possible for every business, regardless of size, to measure better and hold people accountable.

Schilit, Howard, *Financial Shenanigans: How To Detect Accounting Gimmicks and Fraud in Financial Reports* (Second Edition, McGraw-Hill) 2002. ISBN 0–07–138626–2.

From the pioneer of accounting sleuthdom, the common accounting gimmicks and ways to manipulate the financial picture of a company. Use this checklist to evaluate the financial statements of the business you may want to buy.

Stern, Joel, and Donald Chew (editors), *The Revolution in Corporate Finance* (Second Edition, Blackwell Finance) 1994. ISBN 0–631–18554–2.

A compendium of fine articles on the topics of capital budgeting, cost of capital, capital structures, raising capital, interest rate swaps, and spin-offs, carveouts, and divestitures.

Leadership Books

Badaracco, Joseph L., Jr., *Leading Quietly* (HBS Press) 2002. ISBN 1–57851–487–8.

Joe Badaracco is a wonderful, humble leader and professor at Harvard Business School. He graciously helped me when I was beginning my teaching career with no motivation other than kindness. In this book, he dispels the myths of leadership and asserts that leadership is patient, careful, and incremental. He lays out a framework or template for leadership analysis and action.

Bennis, Warren, and Robert Thomas, *Geeks and Geezers* (HBS Press) 2002. ISBN 1–57851–582–3.

The authors look at the role of adversity in a leader's life. They correctly focus on the fact that in extremely difficult times, character, confidence, and values are solidified and that adversity prepares one to deal with life's challenges.

George, Bill, *Authentic Leadership* (Jossey, Bass) 2003. ISBN 0–7879–6913–3.

Bill George is the former Chairman and CEO of Medtronic. His book is an illuminating story about the authentic leadership model. He focuses on purposes, values, and self discipline and gives one hope in this era of corporate scandals that one can lead with values and morals and create shareholder value, too.

Gergen, David, *Eyewitness to Power: The Essence of Leadership. Nixon to Clinton* (Touchstone) 2000. ISBN 0–684–82663–1.

The subtitle of David Gergen's book is "The Essence of Leadership: Nixon to Clinton" and he does not disappoint. A thoughtful work focusing on style, checks and balances, character, and power. My students love this book. The pros and cons of each president's leadership are here for all to learn from.

Goleman, Daniel, Richard Boyatzis, and Annie McKee, *Primal Leadership: Learning to Lead with Emotional Intelligence* (HBS Press) 2002. ISBN 1–57851–486–X.

Goleman and his colleagues at Rutgers and Case Western University have put the leadership onus right back where it belongs—on you and me. Our effectiveness as leaders is dependent on our emotional intelligence. Our ability to manage our emotions, understand others' motions, and to relate and connect to people emotionally. A must read for every male.

Greenleaf, Robert K., *Servant Leadership: Essays* (Paulist Press) 2002. ISBN 0–8091–0554–3.

Robert Greenleaf, a former AT&T executive, in 1977 espoused that service to others was the essence of leadership. Servant leadership is growing in popularity and is also known as values-based leadership.

Books On Lessons To Learn From Bad Leadership

Eichenwalk, Kurt, *Conspiracy of Fools: A True Story* (Broadway Books) 2005. ISBN 0–7679–1178–4.

A spell-binding account of the inner working of Enron primarily from a corporate finance viewpoint. Reads like a mystery thriller. It tells the story of when management loses touch with the details, condones inappropriate behavior, and compensates people for the wrong results. Wall Street's role in this disaster is not pretty. And Arthur Andersen's overriding of its quality control people in order to satisfy Enron is shameful.

McLean, Bethany, and Peter Elkind, *The Smartest Guys In The Room: The Amazing Rise and Scandalous Fall of Enron* (Penguin) 2003. ISBN 1–59184–008–2.

The story of the Enron Company—its culture, value, and leadership. How the greed of the 1990s impacted the ability of accountants, lawyers, and Wall Street to render their duties to the investing public. The story of arrogance, hubris, greed without values, and form over substance. How smart "normal" people got caught up in peer pressure and lost their anchor or compass of what was right and wrong.

Stewart, James B., *Disney War* (Simon and Schuster) 2005. ISBN 0–684–80993–1.

The excruciating details of an autocratic, insecure CEO who packed his Board with those beholden to him. The pettiness, the duplicity, and the failure of core values are mind-boggling. The story is like a soap opera and much can be learned about CEO's decision-making processes.

Management Books

Bossidy, Lawrence, and Ram Charan, *Execution: The Discipline of Getting Things Done* (Crown Business) 2002. ISBN 0–609–61057–0.

Bossidy and Charan refocused U.S. business leadership on the key role of execution. The best strategy in the world is not worth much if you cannot execute it. Bossidy's mantra is a culture of critical inquiry which produces reality for management. His views on constructive debate, measurement, and rewards are spot on. He sets forth the GE model of aligning strategy and action.

Buckingham, Marcus, and Curt Coffman, *First, Break All The Rules* (Simon and Schuster) 1999. ISBN 0–684–85285–1.

This book would have sold even more copies with a representative title. I use it in my classes. It is the best book teaching you how to manage people—how to communicate, set objectives, and hold people accountable, and it is a primer for managing people best practices—based on years of research by Gallup.

Collins, Jim, *Good to Great* (Harper Business) 2001. ISBN 0–06–662099–6.

Jim Collins produced the best-selling business book since *Search For Excellence*. Great concepts here but little about what you do with them—how you create and execute them.

Finkelstein, Sydney, *Why Smart Executives Fail* (Postfolio Books) 2003. ISBN 1–59184–010–4.

Professor Finkelstein's book is a welcomed addition. His research shows that most major business failures occur in big transactions: mergers, change initiatives, new competition, because of leadership's arrogance, hubris, insularity, and flawed cognition—the failure to see and process reality. If you are successful, a must read in order to stay successful.

Magretta, Joan, *What Management Is* (Free Press) 2002. ISBN 0–7432–0318–6.

This book brings all of us back to the basics of what is management. Anytime you get caught up in either management hype or think you have figured the management game out—you should pull this book off your shelf and read it. I do every year.

Sullivan, Gordon, and Michael Harper, *Hope Is Not A Method* (Broadway Books) 1996. ISBN 0–7679–0060–4.

If you need to change something major in your business, read this book about the U.S. Army's massive change initiative in the early 1990s. One of the best books on the execution of change.

Marketing and Sales Books

Bedbury, Scott, with Stephen Fenichell, *A New Brand World: 8 Principles for Achieving Brand Leadership in the 21st Century* (Viking) 2002. ISBN 0–670–03076–7.

From 1995 to 1998 Scott Bedbury was Senior Vice President of Marketing at Starbucks and prior to that, the head of advertising at Nike. Need I say more? A thought-provoking book on the power of brand—what your company represents. An area too frequently overlooked by companies and family businesses. Just maybe your most important product is your brand.

Heskitt, James, W. Earl Sasser, and Leonard Schlesinger, *The Service Profit Chain* (Free Press) 1997. ISBN 0–684–83256–9.

Using Southwest Airlines, Ritz-Carlton, Taco Bell, and others, these three Harvard Business School professors irrefutably establish the link between employee satisfaction and customer satisfaction and loyalty and profits. This book from the logistics and marketing worlds confirms the role of values, people-centric cultures, and employee satisfaction in driving business results.

Kotler, Philip, *Kotler on Marketing* (Free Press) 1999. ISBN 0–68–85033–8.

Northwestern University's Dean of Marketing with over fifteen books to his credit. He views marketing as a competitive advantage and a disciplined strategy. Thought-provoking and will change your view of marketing.

Sheth, Jagdish, and Rajendra Sisodia, *The Rule of Three: Surviving and Thriving In Competitive Markets* (Free Press) 2002. ISBN 0–7432–0560–X.

My friend and colleague, Jag Sheth, has produced the theory that in every industry three companies will dominate a market. The authors give hope to small firms who specialize and who do not get too big to become a target of the Big 3.

ARTICLES

The most consistent source of high quality business articles written for the business person is *Harvard Business Review*. Some of my favorites follow.

Collins, Jim, "Level 5 Leadership: The Triumph of Humility and Fierce Resolve" (*HBR*, January 2001): 66–76.

From *Good To Great*, the Number 1 best selling business book of the last ten years busted the myth about leaders of great businesses. No, they are generally not charismatic larger-then-life heroes. They are humble, passionately-focused people.

Collis, David, and Cynthia Montgomery, "Creating Corporate Advantage" (*HBR* (May–June 1998): 70–83.

How do you align your strategy, structure, control processes, and human resources to maximize your chances of success? Three different models are discussed based on Tyco, Sharp Electronics, and Newell Rubbermaid.

Couter, Diane L., "Sense and Reliability—A Conversation with Celebrated Psychologist Karl E. Werck" (*HBR*, April 2003): 84–90.

I heard Karl Werck talk in February 2005 at one of my conferences about High Reliability Organizations and in 30 minutes he added a whole new dimension to my thought process. Successful organizations not only reward values they cherish, they also focus on non-desired behaviors. This article discusses high-reliability organizations like air traffic controller teams, fire fighters, and emergency rooms.

Drucker, Peter F., "Managing Oneself" (*HBR*, March–April 1999): 64–74.

A wonderful article about the toughest management job in the world—managing yourself. Most people do not spend the time to assess themselves and put themselves into position to play to their strengths. Drucker's "mirror" test is a good one for any leader, parent, or partner.

Magretta, Joan, "Governing The Family-Owned Enterprise: An Interview with Finland's Krister Ahlstrom" (*HBR*, January–February 1998): 112–123.

A thought-provoking interview with the non-family CEO of a large multi-generational family business dealing with issues of governance, the different roles family members play, how to keep the family connected to the business, the roles of Family Councils, and a Family Values Statement.

Miller, Warren D., "Siblings and Succession In The Family Business" (*HBR*, January–February 1998): 22–36.

Three family members vying to be the successor CEO is the recipe for disaster. This Harvard case study is illustrative of the problems of having too many family members working in the business. Four outside experts present their advice. Some practical, some not.

Pearson, Andrall E., "Tough-Minded Ways to Get Innovative" (*HBR*, August 2002): 117–124.

The former President of PepsiCo has more good advice in this seven pages than most books have. He demystifies innovation and growth.

Porter, Michael, Jay Lorsch, and Nitin Nohria, "Seven Surprises for New CEOs"
    (*HBR*, October 2004): 62–72.

A good article for new CEOs of both public and private companies—and yes, family businesses. Generally, CEOs overestimate how fast and how much they can impact an organization. Lessons to be learned—do not think it is about you and do not lose touch with the line employees and customers.

Rogers, Paul, Thomas Holland, and Dan Haas, "Value Acceleration: Lessons From Private Equity Masters" (*HBR*, June 2002): 94–101.

Private equity firms have an expertise in buying firms, operating them for a few years, and either doing an IPO or selling the business at a very good return. Why can these financial engineers run businesses better than management? The authors of the consulting firm Bain & Company studied 2,000 private equity transactions and came away with four key managerial principles that can apply to your business, too.

Slywotsky, Adrian, and Richard Wise, "The Growth Crisis and How To Escape It"
    (*HBR*, July 2002): 72–83.

In the decade of the 1990s, less than 10 percent of the public companies grew their revenues 10 percent or more in eight or more years. Consistent top-line growth is hard. What works? Geographical expansion, acquisitions, price increases, innovation? Their answer lies in your existing customer relationships.

Special Issue: "Inside The Mind of The Leader" (*HBR*, January 2004).

Buy this whole journal. It contains good articles by Warren Bennis (*Geeks and Geniuses*), Daniel Goleman (*Primal Leadership*), Colleen Barrett of Southwest Airlines, and David Gergen.

I use "When Followers Become Toxic" by Lynn R. Offerman in my leadership classes to discuss "Yes People" and "Corporate Suck-Ups."

INFORMATION PORTALS

www.entreworld.org is the information portal of the Kauffman Foundation. Its content is broken down into three parts: Starting Your Business, Growing Your Business, and Supporting Entrepreneurship.

Starting Your Business has nine subtitles:

You, The Entrepreneur; Market Evaluation; Product/Service Development; The Right People; Finances; Marketing and Sales; Legal and Taxes; Technology; and Special Interest Groups.

Under each subtitle are three to seven content areas. Growing Your Business has nine subtitles with three to ten content areas. Critical new ones are accessing capital and growth strategies. The Entrepreneur Search Engine has a wealth of information listed under: Academic Materials, Organizations, Publications, Research, Center for Entrepreneurship, Distance Learning, and Family Business. The Family Business section lists thirty-two Family Business Centers at universities with links to their sites.

www.fambiz.com is the family business portal of Northeastern University. It has a good article search feature.

www.ffi.org Family Firm Institute is a consultant organization that publishes *The Family Business Review*.

www.kennesaw.edu/fec (Cox Family Enterprise Center) is run by my friend, Joe Astraclan. He is the editor of *The Family Business Review* and Cox-published family business cases.

www.knowledge.wharton.upenn.edu is a good, free information source from top-ranked Wharton Graduate Business School.

www.gsb.stanford.edu is the Stanford Knowledgebase and a good, free information source about business thought leadership. Stanford's Executive Education site has an outstanding catalogue of speeches on CD for reasonable prices.

AUTHOR'S COMMENTARIES

These commentaries were written for private company CEOs and owners and the content is explained in the titles. They can be found on my Web site: www.edhltd.com

"The Silver Bullet of Leadership," *The Catalyst*, November 2004.

"Corporate Social Responsibility: The Value of Business Stewardship," *The Catalyst*, October 2004.

"The 'Perfect' Investment," *The Catalyst*, September 2004.

"Entrepreneurs: Reality vs. Myth," *The Catalyst*, July 2004.

"Managing VUCA," *The Catalyst*, June 2004.

"Are Your Employees a Means To Your End?," *The Catalyst*, May 2004.

"10 Keys To Raising Growth Capital," *The Catalyst*, April 2004.

"When Should Your Business Stop Growing," *The Catalyst*, March 2004.

"The Family Business Succession: The Duality Principle," *The Catalyst*, February 2004.

"The Family Business: The Unintended Consequences of Gifts of Stock," *The Catalyst*, January 2004.

"Blocking and Tackling," *The Catalyst*, December 2003.

"What Do Good Leaders Actually Do? (Part II)," *The Catalyst*, November 2003.

"What Is The Meaning Of Business?," *The Catalyst*, October 2003.

"What Do Good Leaders Actually Do? (Part I)," *The Catalyst*, September 2003.

"Do You Have A Broken Arrow Plan?," *The Catalyst*, August 2003.

"Rapid Growth: Be Careful What You Ask For," *The Catalyst*, July 2003.

"Entrepreneurial Leadership: Why Should Anyone Follow You?," *The Catalyst*, June 2003.

"Managing the Family Business: The Golden Goose and the Sandbox," *The Catalyst*, May 2003.

"Going Public To Get Rich: Reality Therapy," *The Catalyst*, April 2003.

"Independent Directors: Private Companies Need Them," *The Catalyst*, March 2003.

"Why Successful Companies Often Fail," *The Catalyst*, February 2003.

"Managing Execution," *The Catalyst*, January 2003.

Index

About the Author

EDWARD D. HESS is an Adjunct Professor of Organization and Management, founder and Executive Director of the Center for Entrepreneurship and Corporate Growth, and founder and Executive Director of the Values-Based Leadership Institute at Goizueta Business School, Emory University, Atlanta, where he teaches courses in entrepreneurship, leadership, and business growth. He also maintains an active consulting practice with family businesses. Prior to joining Emory, he spent over 30 years as a lawyer, investment banker, and consultant, specializing in private family business. He has served as a member of the Carter Center Ambassadors Circle and as a faculty advisor to the Georgia Governor's Leadership Development Task Force. He has written a regular column for the Georgia business magazine, *The Catalyst*; is the author of *Make It Happen: Six Tools for Success*; and co-editor of *Hitting the Growth Wall*.